TALKING
S. H. I. T.

(Social, Humorous, and Inspirational Thoughts)

Jacob Paul Patchen

This book is, for the most part, a collaboration of blog posts from jacobpaulpatchen.com. It has been revised and organized into chapters for your reading pleasure (hopefully).

Published in the U. S. A. by CreateSpace

ISBN-10: 1545510822

ISBN-13: 978-1545510827

For the proud few who can still
remember the Back Road Revival.

Table of Contents

Introduction

We are a strange breed of animal, running around glued to our screens and social medias. We hardly notice anything real anymore. Our friends are a number on a webpage, and the only way that we know if someone is into us, is if they like our post, photo or status. We've become digital. Emotional wrecks of capital letters and emojis. We live and breathe for notifications.

Our knowledge comes from google, not experience. Our rebellions and resistances happen on webpages. We fight people that we don't even know.

Relationships are a battlefield for the loyal and good hearted. We care more about pouty lips and bulging abs than we do about homeless veterans, wars, freedom, and morality. We'd rather make fun of you, than have fun with you. We'd rather tear you down than to let others see our own weaknesses. We'd rather hate, than love.

***

In my epic quest to put my $55,000 of college debt to good use, I started a blog a couple of years ago. I didn't know what I was going to write about, I just knew that I *had* to write.

It didn't take long for my first topic to bloom. I wrote about the life lessons that I learned while growing up just down the hill from my grandpa and his chickens. That first blog post would go on to become my first book, Life Lessons from Grandpa and His Chicken Coop: A Playful Journey Through Some Serious Sh*t.

And then, keeping to the voice in my head of my passionate creative writing professor, *write what you know,* I found myself detailing those late night bar room flings, failings of love, and back road rehabs underneath the stars. I was beginning to tell a social story about a late 20's something, broken man in small town Ohio. I was pushing myself to ask those poetic questions of *why? Why are we here? What are we doing? Why are we so lost and broken?* I was an experienced traveler writing tales about standing still. Hell, I needed to vent.

My blog turned into something more than I had ever thought it would become. It became a message of social humility, of inspiration, of humor, and hope. It raged on my own personal experience of trying to find love, of dealing with the after effects of a war, of a hopeless romantic stuck heartbroken in a crowded room of underdressed drunk girls. It became a place to talk about the ailments that haunt our society; a place to laugh at our gimmicks, to point out our flaws, and to call us out on our bullshit.

I started to write about *us* as a society, through my own faults and experiences. The things that make us move, make us breathe, make us be. I found that we are ridiculously funny at the shit that we try to pull. And it seemed to me that in a world full of booze and broken people, we did all that we could to hide our own stains.

Little did I know that this would not only become a journey about *us,* but more deeply, a discovery about me.

This is a collaboration of my blog, revised and organized into chapters for your reading pleasure.

Buckle up, shit's about to get weird.

First Chapter
Culture

LMFAO!!
(Lick My Face All Over??)

Look, could we pleeeease stop making up new acronyms for every single little phrase that we say on social media.

I'm over here scrolling though different social media feeds, trying to see what all of these strangers have to say, but I can't even begin to creep because they're writing out encrypted code and shit. Like, why do I have to be a Harvard graduate to know what you just said about your cute little kitty cat?

HMU, ROTFL, SMH, AFAIK, AMA, ICYMI, IMHO, LMK, NSFW, YOLO, IDK, IDC, IRL, JK… I mean, WTF?

Alright, don't go getting all butt hurt, I'm not trying to offend you, I'm trying to understand you. Literally. I mean are you actually trying to say something or did you just accidently hit some buttons? Should I know what you mean? Or just guess? Like who determines when we get to make acronyms for phrases? Is there a panel or committee that has to approve it first?? Or do we just throw it out there and let people figure it out? Like, ihniwthytts (I have no Idea what the hell you're trying to say)! Can we just talk normal for a minute? Ya got me over here smdhaotdp (shakin' my damn head all over the damn place).

And what's this "keepin' it 100" crap? Bitch (sorry), that grammatically incorrect and straight up hood rat quote that you just shared doesn't even make sense. How in the hell is anything about that 100%??

 "Idgaf wat nobody say, I boutta do me… mfs gon see. turnt up. 100."

What. In the Hell. Did you just say?

You clearly didn't get a 100% in language arts class, that's for damn sure.

You want to keep it real... you want to keep it "100," then educate yourself in some proper English, and then maybe I can take your gangsta quote seriously. Besides, if you were 100% of anything, then we would already know about it... trust me, you wouldn't need an emoji to let the social media world know. And that little symbol isn't going to convince me of anything either. If you're really that loyal, or hard, or real... then, I'm 100% certain that I'm gonna need to see a little bit more proof than a picture of a red 100. Call me a skeptic, I don't care. I need scientific fact, not some silly little symbol.

Isn't the whole point of social media to communicate... to share our thoughts, and to interact with the internet community? How on Earth does anything that you say have value if I have to decipher the entire encrypted message? I'm over here popping up my urban dictionary typing in random letters just to understand your two sentence status. WTH?!

Look, I'm not trying to hate on anybody for taking a little shortcut every now and then. I understand the concept. Hell, ever since my ICQ and chat room days when I had to BRB because Mom was yelling at me to come clean my room or to put away my laundry, I've been known to throw out the old "LOL" and "LMFAO" as if I had invented them myself (and admittedly, I had no idea what LMFAO meant for the longest time). So don't get me wrong. I understand.

And I get that some social media platforms have a certain "character count" and therefore certain phrases or emojis are appropriate. But, if you're taking the time to share with us all that, "OMG! (oh my God) I'm smdh (shaking my damn head) because my BF (boyfriend) just cheated." And that we should all, "hmu (hit me up) or lms (like my status) because I'm dtf (down to fart?)!!" Then, I need to know exactly what I'm getting myself into when I click the like button beside your "100" symbol. So, please... if you're down to fart... just say so.

Maybe if we would spend a little less time trying to find shortcuts in our communication, then perhaps we'd all be able to understand each other a little better. Maybe we'd be able to relate to one another more wholly, and possibly, feel a better connection and more compassion since we're on the same page. And maybe... just maybe, this lack of clear communication is exactly the barrier that's holding us back....

50 Shades Of Crazy

CRAZY: mentally deranged, demented, insane, senseless, impractical, totally unsound.

Hmm, sounds like the type of girls I seem to go for.

You know, I once had a girl tell me that she loved me more than her on-again-off-again boyfriend, but that she couldn't be with me because he just loved her too much. What?! Then, there are those women who just seem to disappear…the ones you make plans with but then you don't hear from them again until 3 days after you were supposed to hang out. I mean, what the hell? But hey, at least the house gets cleaned and the dishes get done, right?

More recently, I've had a woman ask me when I was going to ask her to hang out (literally 2 days after I had just asked her to hangout, but she was too busy), and then I spend the next 5 days asking her to hang out, but she says that she doesn't like to make plans, and then, like clockwork, all of a sudden she vanishes into the thin air of you're-no-longer-worthy-of-my-reply. Damn it.

Where does this come from? Seriously, when did crazy become the new cool? When did it become acceptable to treat people this way?

Ok, so women are crazy, that's nothing new, we all know that. And if you want to argue with me about it, then I challenge you to observe a woman trying to find something to wear for an important date, or better yet, have a woman explain to you what she looks for in a man and then when "an asshole" doesn't come up on the list, ask her why she's still with that douche who keeps cheating on her or beating her?

But see, that's not even the type of crazy that perplexes me so much. What is really hard for me to understand, is how a woman will want, no, expect a man to treat her with the upmost respect, dignity and compassion, but when a "good guy" is trying to court her, she insists on ignoring them, lying to them, being rude and disrespecting them, and yet, goes on to complain that there just aren't any good guys left out there.

See, I'm confused. How can you have a blatant disregard for, and completely disrespect a decent man, but then go on to question where all the good guys are? Hunny, that's just crazy.

Alright, look… this isn't about bashing women, who are obviously nucking futs… it's about trying to understand why we, as a society, have turned on our values, have taken up the bitter accolades of dishonesty, disrespect, cruelty and rudeness, and then decided that not only will we make this kind of behavior routine, but we will actually celebrate its wickedness and wear it like some shining badge of honor.

I can't count the number of conversations I've witnessed where people (both men and women) are actually amused by how poorly they treat others. I've seen girls literally laugh in a guy's face when he offered to buy them a drink, make fun of him as he walks away, and then later complain because they're not getting enough attention. I've also seen dudes high five each other for getting some tail while their girlfriends were out of town. It disgusts me.

Men aren't innocent. As a gender, we've had a long history of mistreating women. Everything from cheating, to beating, to suppressing, to disrespecting, sexualizing, and harassing, we've done more harm than good. Hell, maybe this is why women are crazy in the first place. Maybe we've forced them to be that way with how harsh we've been in the past. Maybe the sooner we men start treating women better, maybe the sooner they will be able to keep their sanity to begin with.

And hey, look… men are whack jobs, too. Shit, I'll be the first to tell you that I'm crazy. How else could I explain why I keep giving out my heart to people hell bent on destroying it? Look, I'm not perfect, I never will be… but I am courteous, I am kind, I am compassionate, I am loving and caring and gentle. I am decent, and I have to wonder why it's so easy to be so hard on guys like me. We're on your side; we eat, sleep, breathe, live and die for you. So, treat the nice guys better before it's too late, and all the good guys are gone.

I guess, when it comes down to it, what's really crazy, is choosing not to love, but to hate.

The Modern American Slavery

Freedom: exemption from external control, interference, regulation; the power to determine action without restraint; personal liberty, as opposed to bondage or slavery; the absence of or release from ties, obligations, etc. (Dictionary.com)

Liberty: freedom from arbitrary or despotic government or control; freedom from external or foreign rule, independence; freedom from control, interference, obligation, restriction, hampering conditions, etc.; power or right of doing, thinking, speaking, etc., according to choice. (Dictionary.com)

"Give me Liberty, or give me Death," Patrick Henry, 1775.

I am appalled to believe that what we have today is called, Freedom.

We have replaced the chains of slavery with bills, debt, and bad credit. We invite you to the land of opportunity, only to bury you waste deep in a hole of dues, and then hand you a fork to dig your way out.

We tell you to become educated, that a degree will earn you a <u>Million Dollars More</u> than those who don't have one. And so you do, you go, you pick up that pen and take notes, you study for hours and hours (well… some of you), you balance a part time job with full time play, but you still have to take out loans just to get by. And you keep chugging along (sometimes literally) until you find yourself walking across that stage grabbing that certificate (rather quickly) and off you run into the great unknown of money money money… or so you think.

The days pass like summer, fast, loud, and carefree… after all, they give you a full six months until you have to pay back all of that money that you borrowed anyway… shit, life is gravy.

But then, one winter day, you skip out to your mailbox in your fleece robe and ear flap hat, trying not to spill your spiced caramel mocha white chocolate pumpkin vanilla coffee, and as you rip into those still-trickling-in "Congratulations!" letters, you stumble across something odd, something foul, and rancid… a **$1253** bill for your first months payment of your school loans.

You puke, drop your 50 flavors of coffee onto the ground, and briefly consider life as a bank robber.

What the fuck!? This can't be real? Where in the hell am I going to get this kind of money?!

And in those first few moments of bewilderment, dread, and anger… you question everything that you have ever done in your life.

The next few years are Hell. Deferments, Forbearances, lowering your monthly payments, moving back in with your parents, working three jobs so that you can have unlimited data on your cell phone, insurance, a car that drives further than 28 miles, and a new wardrobe of "work clothes". You sacrifice your dignity, fun, and credit so that you can eat more than Ramen noodles and the dollar menu.

Now fast forward to some resemblance of stability five years later.

You have a steady job, an apartment, bills that you can pay the majority of the time, a steady girlfriend/boyfriend, a dog, maybe a kid, a new car, a few suits, a big screen TV, the NFL Sunday Ticket package... hell, you have everything you need.

Except freedom... your job pays $30,000 a year (with your degree) and you have to work 50, 60, and 70 hours a week just to keep the lights on. Your hobbies are napping and job searching.

But you are stuck in Small Town America, where oil and gas jobs are where people sell their life for six figures, and if you want to live comfortably, then you have to live a long, long work week uncomfortably.

And now you are owned by those who pay you. You show up when they say, leave when they tell you, and work as long as they want you to. You cannot do the things that they tell you not to do, or else they will take away your bread. You come and go when they say; you ask permission, and for forgiveness. You wear what they tell you to, their brand, their mark. You do the job that they want, and sometimes more than you should. You say what they want to hear, and you speak in a manner in which they approve.

You follow their rules, their guidelines and their policies, because if you don't, then you will get reprimanded, disciplined, executed from your means to provide. They will end your dreams and fantasies.

Yes, they own you.

Work has become the reason that you live. Without it, they would come and steal your life away.

This is our slavery, this is our captivity… we are workers, dreamers, and wishers. We are the ones who dream of living while we are at work. We are the bound and chained; the confined and broken… we are the working class Americans.

We are so enslaved by the modern world of money, that we freely spend our lives away from our family and friends, new experiences and lessons, home and comfort, just so that we can make the money that we think we need to provide for those things that we do not have the time to do.

Since when did working become the reason that we live?

Whoa whoa whoa, you lazy son of a bitch… How dare you not contribute society! You're a waste of flesh and breath.

What?! No. That's not at all what I am saying.

I'm saying, live. I'm saying… why are we forced to work so hard, so long, so much, for so little? I'm saying… why are we not questioning this idea?

Who came up with a standard 40 hour work week? Fuck… who actually has a job where they only work 40 hours a week, anymore?

Why can't we work 30 hours a week and get paid more on the hour? Hell, why can't we come in for 3 days a week and work really hard for 5 hours to accomplish all that we need to do, and then go home to our family and friends, our experiences and hobbies, our adventures and lessons about life?

Well… if you're looking at these words with a scrunched up face… then you know that it is because of money. Because we are held captive by a piece of paper. Because we sell our lives in order to feel like we are in control of it.

We have become so focused on chasing the American dream, that we have forgotten why we started it in the first place… to be free of worry, to live comfortably, to come home to a *home*, to a family, to live with the ability to experience life.

How much life do you experience working yourself to death?

Wages are too low, too many people are willing to work too long, too hard, for too cheap.

This noble idea of killing oneself in order to provide for the people that they rarely see, is absurd.

Damn it… spend time with the ones you love. Laugh with them, cry with them, be there for them, and experience life with them. Travel, explore, learn, and try new things. Punch through this bubble that you think you are comfortable living in.

Work is not life. Working your life away is NOT living. Why in the fuck do we accept this? Why do we let them control our lives like this? Why do we chain ourselves to a piece of paper that's only real value is in a flame…

We are slaves to those string holders and policy makers. We are puppets that do and say what they want us to.

We are a culture of prude, judgmental, arrogant, flashy, materialistic lost souls who believe that life is about owning things instead of ideas and experiences.

Hell, I don't have all the answers (I'm lucky if I even have one), I don't have the perfect solution, or some easy fix. But I can see our problems; I can see our downfalls, and shortcomings. I think that someone needs to stand up and point them out. I think that we need to raise our voices and speak out. And I think that we need to work together to make our culture better.

So, go do more than just exist. Go be. Go inspire and achieve. Go do the things that make you breathe. Find a way to make us better. And for Fuck's sake... Live.

Halloween Sluts And Creepy Creeps

Well, it's upon us, folks. Another spooky Halloween. The one weekend out of the year where all of the half-naked ghouls and goblins, sexy mini-skirt zombies, and cleavage clad whatchya-ma-call-its, come out to play.

And, let's just be honest, forget about Christmas and Thanksgiving, Halloween has become our new favorite holiday. I mean, what other time of the year is it socially acceptable to go out into the community and put your male parts and lady bits on public display? I damn sure, I don't see Santa Clause or the Easter Bunny doing that shit....

So, here we are, squeezing into our teeny tiny costumes, pushing up our ta-tas, and finding ways to draw attention to our meat sticks. We're cool, we're hip, and we're only doing it to win that $50 Wal-Mart card in the costume contest. I mean, that's what this weekend is really all about, right... Wal-Mart and sex?

Look, ladies, I understand that it's hard to buy a costume that isn't skimpy. Those ass-clowns in the fashion world, the ones who tell us exactly how we're

16

supposed to look, have done a really good job of sexualizing everything. Hell, Halloween doesn't even scare me anymore, because everything that used to want to harm me, now just wants to hump me.

Okay, I guess what I'm really trying to say is… I want to respect you. I want to treat you with class and dignity; as a woman, a man, an adult and a human being, not as a symbol of sexual fantasy and eroticism. But it's hard for me to think of you any differently than that of an attention gathering, "look at me, I'm sexy, because I'm naked," barely clothed, "sex me please," kind of slutty clown that you're acting like.

I mean, how can I even hold a semi-decent conversation with you when every time you "get low, get low" I see your "oh no, oh no?"

And hunny, yes, you are beautiful, there's no denying that… but I think that your nipple is showing. Is that intentional? I mean, should I tell you… or do I just let you figure it out on your own? I really don't wanna make it weird.

"But I'm a slutty pirate."

Yes. Yes you are.

And dudes…. duuuudes… the ones with the body suits and cock socks… what are we doin'? Why is this a thing?? I mean, how proud can you really be?? Personally, I think you look ridiculous, put something else on, please. I understand that it's Halloween 'n' all, but there is absolutely no reason for you to be scaring everyone away like that.

And bro, no. No, she doesn't want you to rub it all over her leg and ass on the dance floor while she's trying to get down with her girlfriends. Just stop. You're embarrassing me, and I don't need your help, I can embarrass myself just fine without seeing any of that. Go try the slutty pirate chick, she looks like she'd dig it.

I understand that we're all here to have a good time; that we all just want to have fun. But listen, we don't really have to advertise our goods this much… do we? We can respect ourselves a little bit, right? Yeah, I get it, you're young and dumb and just wanna have fun. Okay, well good. Me too. But if you're idea of fun is being naked, then hey, be a stripper. At least, then, you'll get paid to have everyone staring at your who-dee-who's and shanaynay's.

But, hey, on the flip side… I really wouldn't mind searching for your (semi) hidden treasure, can I buy you a drink???

Tits And Ass

Sooo, I'm a facebooker. I'll openly and shamelessly admit that. I pay more attention to facebook than I do to my imaginary girlfriend (and let me tell ya, that doesn't go over well at home). I think the thing that interests me the most about the facebook community (other than trying to flirt with people that facebook "thinks I might know") is watching how ridiculous our society has become.

Here's the thing, I'd like to know how many selfies you actually took before you edited, filtered, and posted that fake and deceiving version of yourself? I'm guessing a good handful.

So, why? Why have we become so concerned about the way we look that we are posting fake photos of ourselves on a social network? Do we feed off of those likes and comments? Is that what wakes you up in the morning and lets you rest easy at night… the number of likes and thirsty dudes telling you how beautiful you are (or aren't)???

I'm confused. Seriously, I am. I'm confused about what we, as a society, finds beautiful. It would seem that beauty is no more than a cleavaged clad young lady using some skinny filter and color shading app so that she can look more like the person that she "wants" to be… or, hell, maybe she's just trying to be the person that WE want her to be??

I don't know… but I seriously don't get it… Who have we become? Why is it more important to LOOK good than it is to BE good?

As a single man looking for a potential partner in crime… I can't help but to laugh, shake my head, and feel like we have reached some hopeless point in the evolution of humanity whenever I see a young woman post a skimpy selfie — lips puckered, blowing a kiss to herself in the mirror #nofilter #beauty #love #princess (when you know damn well that she doesn't actually look like that).

Listen, all you beautiful people... yes, you have my attention with your #sexy bikini shots and bathroom selfies... but with that kind of attention, I'm not seeing you as a person, I'm looking at you as a symbol of sex. Is that what you want? Do you just want to be the lust in my eye; the thing I think about when my testosterone soars???

So, you want to get my attention? Okay, good. Post a clever joke, a thoughtful response or solution to some of life's issues... maybe a deeper look as to why we are *here*, what we are doing with ourselves, and who we want to become. At least then I will know that you have the mental capacity to actually think for yourself and be more than just the tits and ass that you post for all of us to see.

Honestly, I don't want to date a stripper (no offence to strippers, I just don't like to share). What I want is an intelligent, funny, clever, thoughtful partner to ponder some of life's biggest questions with. I want a companion who is compassionate, caring, loving, honest, modest and pure.

If you want to get the kind of attention that will really make you feel good about yourself, then try being that kind of person.

And hey, look, if your tits and ass just happen to come along with that, you know, as an added bonus... then hey, I probably just hit the jackpot.

The Dead And The Dying

What has happened to our hometown? What has happened to our friends, our family; our prom dates and teammates, our jungle gym buddies and secret keepers, our brothers, our sisters, our daughters and sons? What is happening to the people that we love?

Folks, what have we done? Why are we not talking about the issues that lead to drug use in the first place? The pain, the anxiety, the loneliness, the heartache, the pressure, and the stress. These are all factors that WE, as a society, can control. They are factors that WE, as a society, contribute. What are we doing to our community?

I mean, I have to ask... is it drugs that are the problem, or is it society? Are we creating an environment that needs escaping from? Are we helping those who need the help? Or are we making life harder for the ones who are already limping?

Look, I'm hardly the guy with the golden answers, but I think that someone needs to start asking the hard questions.

So, whose fault is it then? Is it their fault, the ones who get hooked in the first place? Is it the seller's fault? Or maybe the people who make the drugs?

Perhaps, we are ALL at fault? We as a society have not made living any easier. We hate, we shame, we humiliate, we degrade, and we prey upon the weak to make ourselves look stronger, to make ourselves look cooler.

When are we going to take responsibility for the evil that we induce upon each other?

We are too busy looking for ways to tear someone down, instead of building them up. We are bullies, gangsters, thieves, and tormentors. We'd rather hate each other than to show each other love. WE. ARE. The problem.

And now, hopefully, you're thinking, "What can we do to help? How can we make a difference?"

Well look, there's an old saying that goes something like this, "Be kind, because everyone is fighting a battle that you know nothing about." And that couldn't be more true, especially when it comes to substance abuse.

If we want to stop drugs, then maybe we should first stop giving people a reason to escape? Maybe we should build each other a place of comfort and support; a place full of love and appreciation. Maybe, if we gave them all a reason to stay, then they wouldn't need to go? What I'm saying is, BE THE REASON THAT SOMEBODY WANTS TO LIVE.

And, of course, it's an easier route to just blame them for their addictions, for their problems, for their "weaknesses."

But, don't we ALL, have weaknesses? Don't we ALL trip over obstacles at some point in our lives? Why on earth will we not accept the fact that we all are, ultimately, in the Hurt together?

Listen. You cannot build a bridge without a frame, without support. We are ALL a piece of steel, a piece of iron supporting the weight of each other. And when one beam becomes weak, brittle, tired, and rusted… then it is up to US to bear its weight until it can be repaired. Otherwise, when one beam fails, our entire bridge will fail, and it will fall down hard upon the rocks below.

Folks, we need each other in order to remain sturdy. When will we start acting like it?

Second Chapter

Image

The Perfect Body

I once had a girl tell me that I had the "perfect body"… but not long after that, she passed out into a drunken stooper, drooled all over my pillow and snored for 9 hours straight. When she woke up, she threw up, and then slept/snored for 2 more long, long hours. As I laid there thinking about my perfect body, I realized that the source of this information may not be all that creditable. But later that day, I ran for 2 agonizing miles, anyway.

The perfect body… does that even exist?!?! What the hell is perfect? Shit, even as I sit here, my arms bulging from my midday's workout (well depending on the light and the mirror I look in), I have to wonder, why do I torture myself like I do?

I'm on a schedule, you know… Mondays are chest and back, Tuesdays: abs and run, Wednesdays: bi's and tri's, Thursdays: abs and run, Fridays: body weight, stretch (and drink lots of beer), Saturdays: run and sweat out all the beer, Sundays: rest and wish I didn't drink so much beer all weekend. It's exhausting.

So, why do I do it? Why do I put in the time? Is it pressure? Do I feel like I have to have the perfect body???

I don't think so. Hell, I doubt that I'll ever have the *perfect* body. And, honestly, I could care less. That's not why I do it. That's not why I push myself the way I do. I work out because it makes me feel good, because I like overcoming the pain, because I like the way it makes me feel when I muster up one last shaky rep on one last burnout set. I like the sweat burning in my eyes, the cramps in my muscles as I sprint the last hundred meters. I work out because it's what I've always known. I've always been an athlete and I've always been active. I don't feel like I have to, I feel like I want to. And, no, not for you, but for me. And not because if I don't do it then people will judge me (fuck what people think anyway). I do it because I enjoy it.

Now, let's face it… perfect is subjective. Everyone's idea of perfect is different. For example, I like short blondes who are smart and love to laugh. I would really enjoy a girl who is athletic (as long as she doesn't ever beat me at anything) but quite frankly, I see beauty from the inside. None of those other features would even matter if she didn't have a kind and caring heart, if she wasn't tender and honest, if she wasn't loving and respectful, if she wasn't loyal and moral. I could give a shit less what she looks like if she doesn't possess those inner qualities.

So, here's the question, where does the pressure come from for women to have to have the PERFECT body?!?! I argue that they do it to each other. They're so worried about what "she's" doing, or what "she's" wearing, that "she" looks fat in that top, or "she's" put on a few pounds, or that "she" needs to fix her makeup, that "she" has way too much on or not nearly enough.

Look, WOMEN… you're putting way too much pressure on yourselves. And if you want a man who only wants a woman with a perfect body, then hunny, I'm sorry, but that relationship ain't gonna last. Instead of feeling pressured to look good, feel pressured to BE good. After all, your body is only a symbol of sex, it's your heart that holds a relationship together.

And DUDES… stop objectifying women. A beautiful woman is one that will still be by your side when you're old and stubborn, one that will still put up with your shit even after you're both fat and wrinkly. She's not a beauty contest winner. She's a woman who will always be able to make you smile and laugh, and inspire you to be a better man… no matter if she's gained a few extra pounds or not. She's beautiful because of who she is, not because of what she looks like.

The truth is, the only perfect body we'll ever have, is our body in the eyes of the one who loves us.

Socially Awkward

I'm that dude at social gatherings who doesn't know whether to fist bump or hand shake.

I often get tripped up by the half-a-hug handshake that bro's often do. I sometimes creep into social circles at parties and laugh at the first thing said so that I fit right in. And then I say something stupid like, "Hey, I just read an article about how they discovered 10 new exoplanets and that one may even be able to support life…." Yeah, I say weird, awkward shit, but by no fault of my own. I can't help it. I'm just not good at being cool in social situations.

Sometimes, I bring up politics when we are out at the bar. Why? Hell, I'm not real sure. It just seems like more people should be worried about their right to live freely.

The truth is, I never really know what to talk about. I have no idea what the Kardashians are doing. What Bieber jam is hot right now, or if he's even important anymore. I don't know what happened on The Bachelor or The Bachelorette… and I don't understand why they don't just hook those two people up in the first place. I mean, they've gotta have mutual friends within the network, right?

I never know if someone wants to hug me, kiss me, or punch me in the face. And that makes it hard for me to feel comfortable when we're all together. I mean, just imagine, trying to hug someone who wants to punch you in the face.

My friends never seem to have any problem fitting in. They walk into a crowded room and know right away who they're going to fight, buy a drink, or dance with on the dance floor.

Nope. Not me. I'm over here in the corner, where it's safe, watching and waiting (probably like a creep) hoping that some decent looking gal gives me an obvious sign that they are interested. And by obvious, I mean, walk up to me, rub my shoulder, and whisper something into my ear like, "Hey cutie, you don't have to do a thing, I'm all yours."

That's how it works right? I mean, it seems that easy for my crowd pleasing, life of the party, rowdy friends. So, what class did they *mostly skip* that taught them how to be this social? Where did they learn how to interact so easily?

Shit, I'm usually six beers and 4 shots of tequila deep before I'm finally out there on the dance floor getting weird. But they walk into the club, buy a beer for each hand, and leave me at the bar while they go make friends with the slutty girl droppin' it low.

But I'm the shy, cute one. I mean, there are those days. But that's not really who I am. There's a God Damned lion inside of this gazelle! A very talkative lion, who always knows what to say. One that never experiences those long moments of awkward silence. A lion who struts out into the open, his long beautiful mane flaring in the savanna sun, drawing in all the eyes of the African plains, looking important, being heard and seen, owning that shit.

Yes, there's a lion inside of me.

He's just... drunk right now.

It's Not Called Balding, It's Called Maturing

Well, it's been nearly a year, now, since I made the executive decision to buzz my head and rid my tiring locks of their honorable responsibility of making me look younger and more fertile. The struggle was real.

But, just recently, I decided to un-retire my dirty blondes in a reunion of youth, hope, and spiked bangs. But, despite my dismal efforts to reignite the flame of passion that was once my high and tight... my frail, feeble hair returned to not even half of its former self.

So, this morning, despite objections from that hopeful little voice in the back of my head (who is probably intoxicated, because, let's face it, he'd have to be well on his way to wasted in order to be THAT hopeful), I conceded, and shaved what pitiful effort it was to bring sexy back, back off of my head.

I suppose that it's just time to face it... I'm a balding man.

What's that you say!!??

Yes… yes, I am starting to get smooth up top and shiny in the back. How the HELL did this happen!!?? Well, to be honest, (and I mean completely honest) I think it was a plot to sabotage my "sexiness", orchestrated by inferior single men who obviously felt threatened by my golden rays of hair shine. Yeah! Yeah! That's what it was… I was drugged, damn it! They stole the finely crafted masterpiece on top of my head and moved it down to my back. Those assholes!!

Okay… okay… back to reality. So, I've come to terms with what's at hand. After all, it's not balding… its MATURING.

Hell, just the other day I checked my bank account before I made an, absolutely, unnecessary purchase. Seeee, MAA-turity. You know, back in my younger, more bushy days, I would have thought, EFF what the bank says, and I'd have overdrawn my account just because I could. Oh, and yesterday, I think it was yesterday… I did a couple of chores!! YUP, I cleaned up a few messes around the house, I made my bed (which reminds me, that I need to wash the sheets), and I even did the dishes… well, sort of… I mean, I went ahead and threw away the ones that we undo-able. Close enough.

Alright, balding isn't exactly a baaad thing… you have no idea how many people have told me that I look just like that Daughtry guy. And, hey… we all know that Daughtry is a sexy mother trucker. Am I right, or am I right?? High fiiive!

Yyyeah… so anyway, what I'm saying is… there's no need to flip over couches and tear down walls just because you're losing your hair. In fact, you should probably clean the couch and wipe down the walls, because, well, balding men are classy and apparently get way more ass than the seat of J-Lo's pants.

Look, balding doesn't make you any less of a man (well, maybe a little shorter) but you are still YOU. Just because you have to wear a hat more often, doesn't mean that you are more of a sissy, now. No, some of the strongest people I know are bald… like Stone Cold Steve Austin, or Goldberg.

The truth is, what makes you a man is how you treat others, it's how you carry yourself, the respect you give, the compassion you show, and the amount of love that you hold in your heart… not the amount of hair on your head.

Besides…. from what I've been told, bald men make better lovers, anyway.

Who Are You

No, seriously, who are you?

I mean, of course, you're a name. You're a mother, a brother, a father, a sister, an uncle, an aunt, a friend, and a lover. You are a man or a woman (or maybe both, who's judging). You are a sinner or, hell, a product of evolution. You are like, 60 to 80 percent water (I think). You are flesh. You are bone. You are movement in the space of time.

But who are *you?*

How often do you really think about it?

How often do you think about the person that you want to be; the person that you were, or the person you've become?

Hell, for me, it's daily. And I don't know if that's normal, nor do I really give a shit. But the fact still remains, that even in my 30's, I'm still learning who I am.

Now, I don't know how old you are, but I can assure you this: no matter what age you are, from teens to your 90's, knowing who you are will always be important.

And right now, you're like, *No shit, Jake. Now tell me something less stressful that I don't already know.*

Alright, well… You. Will. Change. **A lot**, in your lifetime.

But here's what I want to know: **What makes you important?**

For the love of God, if you do not know, then drop everything that you are doing, right now, (well, okay, after you finish reading) and go figure it the fuck out.

After all, if you don't know why you're important, then what purpose do you have?

I want you to have a purpose. I **need** you to have a purpose. *Youuu* need you to have a purpose.

So what makes you breathe?

The touch of your lover's hand? The laughter of your kids? The 4 a.m. barking of your dog child on a Wednesday morning? Food? Wine? Sex? The Bachelor season finale?

For me, it's the hope, the faith, the adventure, the reality, and fantasy of love. It's the stirrings inside of me that forces an ear to ear grin, even when I'm trying to be mad at her. It's the higher pitch in my voice when I say *babe.* It's the gut busting laughter of chasing each other around the house with nerf guns, popping around corners like I was back in the Marines, groucho-ing down the hallway, heel-toe, heel-toe, waiting for her to come into view. It is the tickle fight that ensues. The strip poker, strip scrabble, strip bets on football games and scores. It's the fact that I can make her laugh when she is mad. Or that I can say the words that connect the world for her when it is nothing but shattered. It is the words that I write, the dreams that I wake her up to tell. It is the morning. The night. The stars. The sky. The back roads. The lake. The summer sounds around a campfire. The sneaking off into the darkness to kiss her forehead, her lips, her neck. It is the feeling that lets me know that life is meant to be lived; that we are here to feel.

I am hope and faith, love and mercy, joy and hate, sadness and pain. I am the things that make us move.

And my purpose, is to do just that.

Third Chapter
Love

Finding Love In A Bar

There you are, in what you think is your lucky shirt, sitting at the bar laughing, drinking and having a good time with your buddies, when all of a sudden, you look up and happen to notice some beautiful little thing standing off in the corner with some of her friends.

Now, the loud one with the low top you've seen before, but not her, not this one. No, this attractive, awkwardly-out-of- place angel standing right over there swirling her still full glass of pink drink, you've never seen before. You start to get excited. But, she catches you staring and you nearly choke on your heart. You dart down to your drink. *Shit*, you think, *real cool*. So you try to look out of the corner of your eye. Is she still looking? You can't tell, so you turn your head and meet her gaze. But this time, she's smiling. So, you smile back, then panic, and raise your drink to a toast. She laughs, and does the same.

The rest of the night you spend telling her how ready you are to find a good girl and settle down. She tells you that she's a nurse and wants to change the world. You hit it off as if it were meant to be, and laugh the night away.

But the next morning she texts you to say that she's sorry, but she was just drunk and is getting back with her ex-boyfriend.

Hell, it happens more times than you think it possibly could… and yet, there you are, every Friday and Saturday night, in another one of your damn lucky shirts, buying drinks, getting drunk and trying to convince some pretty little thing that you honestly, truly, seriously, really are a good guy.

But to no prevail. You're still single. You're still heartbroken time and time again. So, WHY? Why do you still think that somehow, someway… in some distant magical fucking universe that you will meet the love of your life at some stinky, sticky, life-sucking little bar?!?!

Well, it's quite simple, really.

You have CONVINCED yourself that this is where people like you come to meet. You think, hey, I'm a good guy, I'm dateable, I'm decent, I'm loving and caring and respectable… so, if I'm here looking to meet someone new, then there's bound to be some wonderfully charming, sweet young woman out there in the loud crowd of low cut tops and too many shots looking just for me.

Dude. W.T.F. are you thinking? Yes, you want a girl who has the same hobbies as you. Yes, you want her to be fun and drink and dance and be social with all your friends… but, look here…Good. Girls. Do Not. Go Out. To a Bar. To Meet Their Future Husband. It's that simple.

Ok… ok… so there are some exceptions to the rule. Yes, it's happened before. There's always that one couple who's sooo happy that they're friends drug them out of the house on that one special night so that they could meet the one true love of their life! Alright. Good for them. But, dude… dude… seriously. You've been in the game long enough to know that, #1 any good girl that is out drinking is out to simply have a good time with her friends, a.k.a. she's NOT interested in you… #2 how charming and sexy can you really be slurring your words and smelling like stale beer… and #3 her parents will hate you already.

So, what's a guy to do? Hell, you've already invested thousands of dollars, moments, and pick-up lines, right? So, now what?

Well, you could always clean yourself up a little, be more friendly, donate some of your time to helping others, walk with your head up and shoulders back, smile more, laugh as much as possible and hope, and pray… that someday, somewhere (but hopefully here in this magical fucking universe), some beautiful, light hearted savior will care just enough to come and save your soul.

And if not… then, go grocery shopping every chance you get.

A Night Of No Regrets

"I'm going to the bathroom." She announced to the room, as she stood up from the couch across from me. But, before she disappeared around the corner and up the stairs, she shot me a look that invited me to find a reason to follow her. Then, she vanished up the steps. I counted the seconds until it was safe for me to say that I needed to piss, too.

"Damn, now, I've got to go, too." I said without really giving a shit what they read into it. I headed towards the stairs in the best drunken shuffle that I could muster, trying to make them believe that I was too intoxicated to realize how close behind her I actually was.

It worked. They had no reason to believe that our plan was to get away from them. They were all drunk chatting with drinks in their hands, some kind of watching TV, kind of not, jumping into the conversations here and there. They had no idea that we just had to be alone.

The moment was ours; just two friends who have fallen into the grasp of love. And, though, we were so wrong, we felt so right. We weren't about to let what little time we had slip away.

I reached the top of the stairs where I met her gaze from inside the bedroom. She was lying on her side facing me with a look that shouted "sexy". I couldn't fight it, no matter how hard I tried; she was the only reason that I bailed on my friends tonight. But I didn't really regret it. And I didn't know that it would go this far. And I damn sure didn't anticipate this happening, either. I just wanted to be near her, to smell her, to hear her voice, to see her smile. I just wanted to know that she was thinking of me when we were ten feet away hiding our feelings from our friends.

I entered the doorway and shut the door behind me; there was no way that I was going to let them hear us. I didn't count the strides it took me to make it to the bed, nor, did I count the seconds that it took for me to strip the clothes from my body, but I know that mere moments were all that I allowed to pass by.

I reached the bed in an anxious kind of way, like when a child wakes up on Christmas morning and rushes to the Christmas tree; she was my Christmas tree, my present, and I just had to unwrap her, I just had to get my hands on the gift that was waiting for me underneath of that smiling bow of hers.

My fingers find her in the darkness, then my eyes adjust and I can see her faint, nude silhouette. The moonlight shines through her bedside window and touches the far corners of the room; I can see her face now. The smile that greets my eyes sends a burst of blood through my entire body. I want to say something charming, but words aren't necessary; we both know what we want and there's no reason to say it. Instead, we play it out.

The TV downstairs sends laughter through the closed door. We unravel our bodies in fear of being caught, but quickly chuckle at how cautious we are. My lips search the darkened space between her face and mine until I decide to press them against her lips. The warmness boils my blood, and I shutter, feeling that familiar tingle of goose bumps. My mind explodes with reasons why I should and shouldn't feel this way, but, quickly, they are chased away by the diction in her voice.

"I don't understand why you like me so much."

"Who said I like you at all." I tease with a smile.

"I wish you'd just open up to me."

I pause in thought. "If I admit it, then I won't be able to turn back." I say softly.

"But I'm giving so much, I tell you everything. I even talk about him." She pleads.

I take that comment to heart. "The things I want to tell you aren't supposed to be said in our situation. Because, once I say it out loud, the things I feel, then there's just no turning back."

"I don't care," she confesses. "Just for tonight, I want to pretend that this ring isn't on my finger." She stares straight into my eyes, straight into my heart.

And I can't help it…

"I love you, Jeanna."

Crazed, Desperate, Love Desperado

Love, where the hell are you?!

I've been looking for you for months, now. I've been down to the supermarket, dressed in my fancy clothes, wearing my expensive cologne, I even shaved (well, sort of, I trimmed and tamed my wild and beautiful beard). I walked around for hours following potential lovers down stocked grocery aisles, pretending that I needed more pasta or carrots or whatever that mixed bag of healthy green shit was; I did that for you. But you ignored me. I smelled good, but you kept on walking by, as I sifted through the mangos, feeling for their firmness (like I know what the hell a mango is supposed to feel like anyway), but you weren't impressed. No, you headed straight for the meat section and mingled with the gentleman picking out T-bones; *hmm I want a T-bone*. Hell, I'll buy you a T-bone. I'll buy you *three*, one for breakfast, lunch and dinner.

Shit, I'm trying too hard!

But how do you not try for something that you need. Oh, there's my problem right there, I need you, Love. What horseshit! Love, you need ME!! Because, I still believe in you. I still honor and respect you, hell, I still put you on a pedestal… because that's exactly where you belong, up above the rest, for all things to admire and cherish. But they don't… Love, they don't cherish you. They trample you, they take advantage of you, they deny you, they lie to you, cheat on you, spit in your beautiful face… that is, until they no longer have you. Then, they talk about you like you were best friends… like you and them would go to the park and lay on your backs, looking up at the sky, and just talk for hours about the interworkings of life. Love, you're underappreciated.

Well, here we go.

I had you, Love… and then I lost you. You shit on me, and I shit on you… what a strange relationship we keep; as if we are phases of the moon, we have our bright nights and those that are dim. But, Love… I appreciate you like I do the moon; like that time we sat out by the lake, watching that golden circle arch up over the horizon. It inspired us didn't it?? It inspired us to start a fire, to strip down to nothing and wade out into the cold calm waters of the unknown. You and me made one hell of a splash that summer. Do you remember? Can you still feel the excitement of me chasing you around in the water? Can you still feel my body pressed up gently against yours, slightly trembling, as we held each other in circles under the light of the moon until we were wrinkly and cold? But then, up on that bank, we stoked that fire, bringing those coals to flame.

I miss that. I miss that warmth you brought me, Love.

You know, they say to be patient, that you will catch up to me eventually. But, how can I believe them when they have also chanted, "Love is Dead." Love, you are NOT dead. Wounded, perhaps… laying in some cold, dark corner of some enchanted forest, bleeding out, crying out… "Save me! Save me! Save me!"

Love, be strong… I'm coming for you!

Finding The G Spot

FYI: For those of you who don't know, I often reach out to my Facebook friends for topic ideas. It's not that I lack the creativity to come up with my own (I think I'm actually winning so far if we put it to a count), but I like to get my friends and "fans" involved. It works like this: people throw out topic ideas and whichever idea gets the most likes, that's the one I write about. And, well, I like to stick to my word, so... today's topic is inevitably going to be about "the G spot... where is it really located?"

Now, without any further FYI's, I think that I'll just go ahead and remove all barriers, and try to penetrate deep inside this mysterious myth, fantasy, folklore, FACT, with every intention of aiming to please.

The G Spot... the Good Spot... the Great Spot... the "Oh, G...G...GOD!!" Spot.

First of all, and for the sake of this blog post, let's just assume for a second that I've actually had sexual intercourse (although, if some of you young, brazen, fellows venture to dispute this claim, then, I encourage you, please, just go ahead and ask your mother).

Now, where was I? Oh, yeah... about to dive head first and hard into this G Spot thing.

Through extensive research (ok, ok… I googled it and clicked on the first thing that popped up), I've discovered that this infamous pleasure zone actually does exist… even if you haven't found it yet. Apparently it's a quarter sized, spongy tissue area that's located about one to two inches inside the vaginal opening on the front vaginal wall (by "front" I mean the same side as the "milk-makers"). Again… that's one to two inches inside the front of the vagina. So, fellas, even the Unfortunate shouldn't have a problem locating this area; all you need to do is just put in "a little" effort.

Okay, so it actually exists, I mean, I found it on the internet, so it has to be true, right? (But just between me and you, I already knew that. And, for those women who dispute my knowledge of such, I assure you… I was purposely going around it. It's not me, it's you).

But, you see, here's where I differ… ladies… gentlemen… and G Spot enthusiasts… the REAL G SPOT… is not down south, it's up north.

What I mean is… the good sex, the REALLY GOOD SEX… that's when you penetrate her mind, her heart, and her soul. The best sex I've ever had (was with myself) no, no, no, no… the best sex… isn't just sex… it's MAKING LOVE!

Let me say that again… the best sex you will ever have, isn't on some fantasy check list (well, unless it's with me, obviously)… the best sex is located inside your head, inside your heart; it's soul shaking, it's "Good God, I love this woman/man" kind of sex. It's "I want to give everything to you, I want to be everything for you, I'd die for you," kind of sex.

People, the real G Spot is a quarter sized, spongy little area of YOU, located one to two inches inside of her heart (her metaphorical heart, not her literal heart… you creeps).

So, I insist, gentlemen, stop trying so hard to "hit the right spot," and instead start focusing all that time (38 seconds) and energy (14 calories) on loving **her**, on being there for **her**, on showing **her** exactly how much she means to you. Because, I promise you… if you don't… then I will. And trust me… I can find both G Spots…

Our Most Distant Week

You're lying on the couch watching TV, and I'm in the other room writing on the computer.

I can hear the laughter of Impractical Jokers, and you, whose distinct *hehehe* is nearly as visible as that toothy smile that always goes along with it.

I would normally be sitting beside you, holding onto you, jabbing at your sides with my finger, tickling you, trying to make that laughter go on forever.

But I'm not.

I'm giving you, no… I'm giving *us* the space that we need after our moody weekend; after this distant and distracted, wall building, insecure week.

You have no idea that I'm in here writing about you. And I don't expect to tell you. I suppose you will find out one night when you pick up this book for the first time, and read it.

I'm sorry.

I think that I should start with that. Because, quite frankly, I don't know what the fuck happened.

I guess that's what makes two broken people so fragile, the unraveling of one nerve that leads us to hold on for dear life, and then retreat back into the caves of comfort and loneliness that we came from.

Did I say something wrong? Probably.

I mean hell, I can't breathe without blowing flames on most of those nights after work. Flopping around convulsing, mumbling incoherent gibberish about how social work, and that controlling, power hungry-she-devil-bitch is sucking the life right out of me and my clients. You must feel the heat from that fire. And I am sorry.

Work is the bandit of love; calling *you* in at night, emailing *me* rage, consuming **our** time together. I dream about saving the world, when I used to dream about saving you. Hell, maybe I just need you to fall apart again in order for me to be your hero…

I don't know when I lost the sanity in my life, but I know that it is gone.

I mean, listen to me rambling on like some fucking idiot about work and you and me and us and then and now and when and how. And Fuck. What is this, Days of Our Lives?

I just wanted to tell you that I miss you.

Not in the soap opera, mushy, dramatic, sweep you off of your feet and kiss you loudly for hours kind of way, no… I miss you leaning on me, I miss you *hehehe-ing* at my random dumb shit, our break out dance parties, one on one drunk strip poker nights, the noises that you make while you sleep next to me, your messy hair when you wake up and put it in a loose bun, the way that you shiver with emotion when I pull you in close, your pale butt cheeks when you disappear into the bathroom after making love.

It's been <u>one</u> emotionally distant week, and I feel like you've been gone for <u>months</u>.

We sure as shit don't have to be perfect, but know that I want you, I miss you, and I still want to be your hero.

Forth Chapter
War

10 Years Ago I Wanted To Kill You

There is a Demon tied to a stake deep down in the darkest corner of my soul; and 10 years ago, I sliced him free with a Ka-Bar knife.

***

For those of you who knew me back in my younger days, you all are probably nodding your head "yes," right now. You must've had the unfortunate pleasure of dealing with that baby demon (while babysitting, or in church, or wherever) back before I had whipped him into his corner. I apologize. With my deepest, most sincere apology, I – Am – Sorry.

And for those of you who have no idea how big of a temper tantrum my 8 year old self could throw… consider yourselves the lucky ones. Because, luckily for everyone opposed to temper tantrums, phone throwing, running away, and other mischievous acts, I buried that son of a bitch a long time ago…

But 10 years ago today, I cut him loose.

***

What going to war does to the mind is astonishing. To convince myself that taking another person's life is right, was difficult to do. And accepting that they could possibly take mine, was even harder to do. But I did. I switched whatever human psyche switch I needed to in order to kill and/or to be killed.

I went as far as to write a death letter that was meant to be sent home if I was killed in action. I still have it. And, occasionally, I revisit it, and try to remember the love, fear, and appreciation for life that I felt as I wrote those shaky, sweaty, and tear stained words.

To be honest, it amazes me that it was never mailed. Even though they had their many chances, for some reason... I just wasn't called home.

But, Joey was.

He was my squad's 1st team leader. He was good at what he did. He was kind hearted and just. He had a sense of humor that would change your day. He was cool, he was good, and he was a brother to us all.

We were at an outpost called the B/U Split. It was an intersection for a "civilian only" road and a "military only" road. Simply put: we were there to keep the bad guys from driving onto the "military only" road, where they could rig up I.E.D's and landmines.

Not much happened out there, honestly. I think those sandbagged bunkers took fire 1 time during the whole time that we were there. So, we were slightly more "relaxed" than anywhere else we had been, so far. Hell, I think we even played a game of baseball with some rolled up duct tape for a ball, a time or two.

We were supposed to be a on 2-3 week rotation with the other platoons. While there, we did 8 hours sitting on post watching traffic and looking for suspicious behavior, and then 8 hours off post resting or whatever. We would watch movies from a generator on our down time, write letters home, look at stolen girlfriend pictures that some idiot forgot to put away, read magazines, shower from a water bottle and sleep when it was cool enough to do so. What I'm trying to say is, in the hell hole, shit storm of a landmined, IED'd, rocketed and pop-shoted world that we found ourselves living in during this deployment, this was the one place where nothing was supposed to happen.

But it did.

Lights were reported the night before about a mile or two out at some abandoned stone buildings in the desert. So, the next day, the order was given to do a mounted patrol out to these buildings and check it out. But, by the time that they had everything finally approved, it was time for me to stand my shift of post. I wasn't able to go with them, and I was pissed.

We flipped each other the bird as they headed out of the wire, everyone joking and smiling, ready to go do what we get paid to do; find the bad guys and eliminate them. I watched them stop traffic and slowly head down the road with their gunners sweeping their sectors of fire. I was envious; I hated post.

***

That was the last time that we would all be together. It was the last time that I would see Joey's smile, as he made fun of me for having to stand post instead of going out on patrol with them.

His Humvee hit a landmine, throwing them all into the air from its opened back.

Gunny and I ran, as fast as we could go, together, down that same road that traffic was still stopped on, in our full gear, dying inside the closer we got to that black smoke cloud.

I'll never forget my brothers laying there in the sand, the Corpsmen over top of them, trying to patch them up.

I'll never forget the rage that swelled up inside of me as I felt the pain in their screams. I'll never forget the fear, and the fever that boiled over from knowing that things would be different now... that no longer will our demons stay chained in the corner.

I WANTED TO KILL YOU!

Whoever you were, wherever you were, hiding, blending back into the crowds of innocent people. I wanted to find you, to cut you open, and to watch you bleed like my brothers were right in front of me.

That's the first, and the last time that I have ever let my Demon out of that darkness…

They say that time heals all wounds. I don't know, maybe it does. But 10 years has not healed that pain.

A Veteran's Sacrifice

First and foremost, from the bottom of my humbled heart, I want to thank all Veterans for their willingness to sacrifice for my freedom, protection, and peaceful way of life. Thank you.

For the last 2 weeks I've anticipated this post with angst. The idea of capturing the meaning of Veteran's Day: what it means to be a Veteran, what it feels like to share that honor with so many other glorious men and women, the gratitude for their courageous sacrifices, the appreciation and understanding of what they had to go through to protect our freedom and peace of mind; it seems too big of a feat for me to handle. And I go into this knowing that a few long paragraphs will, most certainly, come up short.

But, if I don't write something, though, only mere words… words that, to many, will lack an understanding, a connection, or clarity, because they have not lived through the kind of hell that we have savored; if I do not try, then I have done nothing but disgrace those heroes who were willing to give everything for me to have the ability to sit here in the comfort of a peaceful home, in the sanctuary of a free Nation, and write these earnest words.

*** I've stared at this blank space for over an hour now. There's so much I want to say but no meaningful way to say it.

SACRIFICE. The word is engraved into the heart of a Veteran. It's as real as writing your will before you deploy; as sobering as trying to remember what you actually have worth value, at the age of 19, that you would want your family to remember you by: the .22 rifle that would go to your younger brother because he needed a new one, the 870 12 gauge shotgun that would go to your older brother because he was a horrible shot, the love letters and secret knickknacks that you would want your girlfriend to keep. It's taking 20 minutes out of your "gear prep time" in order to quickly jot down your own death letter in case you were the one to hit that next landmine or I.E.D. It's the "I love you's" that you didn't quite say enough before, but now, realizing that this 5 min satellite phone call back home before a 17 day "Op" might be the last time that you ever hear your mom and dad's voice again, so you say it 3 times before you hang up.

The stories of sacrifice and heroics on the battlefield are endless. But I lack the ability and the talent to tell them justly. Instead, I want to dedicate the remainder of this post to those metaphorical gashes and scars that still bleed and stay with us long after we return home.

I'm talking about the changes in perception… when a pile of trash along the road goes from "a pile of trash" to "a possible I.E.D. explosion," when a person with a cell phone goes from "innocent" to "a spotter for incoming mortars and rockets," the jerk of adrenaline and reflex to "take cover" at the BOOM of any loud noise. I'm talking about the thousand-yard-stare, combat look in my brother's eyes the day I had to put him into a choke hold in order to pull him off of some ignorant low life trash who started a fist fight with our friends. I'm talking about the scars on my knuckles from the time I put my fist through a window to relieve my pain and frustration of another girl not being able to love the person I had now become.

Like many other Veterans, I keep a firearm near me as I sleep. The comfort of knowing it's there when I wake up from some noise inside of my house, or inside of my nightmares, is worth more to me than what you could ever possibly understand. A man without a way to defend himself… is a dead man. A Marine without his weapon… is useless. It's a philosophy and mindset that was only enhanced by the spoils of war. Kill, or be killed. KILL, because if you hesitate, then you are a liability to the safety of your squad. KILL, because that is your job, that is what you are here to do, to kill the enemy, to stop them from killing you or your brothers or other innocent men, women, and children.

And the toll for accepting this responsibility to take a life is grand. To convince your mind, no... your heart, that it is acceptable to end a person's life is a demanding task. But, to actually contemplate, to rationalize and inevitably accept that at any moment, your life could end in fire and smoke, or perhaps from some distant trigger pull and pop of some coward who will surely slither away into the shadows... accepting that death, and living with that acceptance... is a gross burden to endure. But we do. We weather that storm.

To get a taste of the mental toll Veterans pay, sleep in a room full of Marines post deployment.

I've been witness to countless screams of fear and fits of rage from sleeping Marines. I've actually witnessed a Marine stand up in his sleep, kick his leg into the air, point his empty arms forward and scream "get some fucking light on that room!!" Then, he laid back down, asleep, as if nothing had even happened. And personally, during one nightmare, I've felt the blood drain from a shrapnel wound in my neck. The feeling was so real that I woke up kicking and screaming holding pressure on the imaginary gash in my jugular. These are just a small fraction of the stresses that Veterans face on a daily basis. And they absolutely have a lasting effect.

The suicide rate for Veterans is 22 a day. Twenty-two Veterans a day, who made it through combat, come home and commit suicide. It's an unbelievably tragic reality that these 22 Veterans every single day, feel that their life is no longer important enough to remain existent. I'm shakingly reminded of the handful of Marines from my Company who ended their lives after our tour to Iraq. Or the time that a buddy of mine called to talk because he just pulled the handgun out of his mouth and decided not to pull the trigger "this time." Without a doubt, these are the hardest tragedies to understand.

When I think of Veterans Day, I think about the constant troubles that these brave men and women endure daily because they chose to dedicate their life to defending ours.

What could be more worthy of a simple "thank you" than that?

A Marine's 4th Of July

As the 4th of July is upon us, I can't help but to think about where we would be if we did not have people like the ones I served with, to stand up for our beliefs and protect our Constitution and freedoms. I am truly forever grateful for those men and women, and will always remain in their debt. I think back to past 4th of July's and, to be honest, they all sort of just blend together into a drunken weekend festival of good times and laughter... except for one; July 4th, 2005. It was spent with my brothers in the hot, nasty, hostile, shithole, known as, Iraq.

Now, I've never minded sharing my experiences with anyone that was curious, even if they'd never truly understand. I feel like people should hear as many stories about combat as possible. Unfortunately, after 9 years, some of the details of those stories are a bit clouded. But, luckily for all of you, or maybe me, rather, I actually kept a journal of my deployment (even through the harsh ridicule and numerous jokes). So, in honor of all of those who are serving away from their families in harm's way, protecting our way of life... I will share with you my thoughts and experiences from July 4th, 9 years ago, outside the city of Hit, Iraq at the B/U Split post.

(Disclaimer: this journal entry jumps around a bit as it tries to capture what life was like out at this tiny remote post in the middle of the nowhere that was meant to keep civilian traffic off of a "military only" road. We had already done numerous missions up to this point; anti-insurgent patrols, road security, house searches, anti-mortar patrols, weapons cache patrols, and ambushes, but this was a "sort-of-relaxed" job where we were out of the brunt of the fight for a short while. We had been there for 3 weeks already and were pretty bored.)

Monday July 4, 2005 (20 years old)

It's hard looking back, now, and thinking about what all the men and women who fought for our freedom had to go through. I've hardly touched the surface of what they must have seen and done. It's an understanding that only men who fight and die can know. And it's a great honor to just be a part of that breed of men!

Well, we actually played homerun derby out here for the last 2 days but I hurt my back even more. I must have pulled something. I guess I'm out of shape from 3 weeks on post.

Lee Roy just threw chem-lite all over me after I told him not to. I jumped up pissed off and shoved him (wish I would've punched him), but now, I'm just pissed.

The guys keep running their mouths and its pissin' me off. I'm tired of always being the nice guy. They take advantage of me for that because I refuse to stand up and fight them while we're in a combat zone. And as badly as I want to, they are not the enemy. We can't fight each other and expect to win the fight against these dirty, cowardly, bomb making bastards. Hell, I suppose we're just all sick of standing post instead of getting back to kickin' in doors.

So, anyway, we've had a few more explosions the last couple of days. We haven't really heard much about anything really, though. And now, the latest rumor is that India is coming out in a few days, so, maybe we'll go into Hit or maybe we'll just stay at the FOB, we don't know yet.

The more and more time that goes by, the more we thirst for blood. It's a horrible thing how much I want to kill. With the chain of events that have happened while we were here, the more shit that happens, the mortars, the rockets, the IED's, landmines and random pop shots… the more we go through… the more we just want to kill. I'm turning into something that I hate, something that only knows hate. And it's, honestly, just fucking scary.

END

***

That night Gunny set off 3 pop-up-flares in celebration of the 4th. Of course, we only had red, white, and green… so it was only mostly patriotic. But it took us all back home, if for only a few seconds. And, honestly, those were the best damn fireworks that I have ever seen in my life.

But unfortunately, thanks to all the mortars, rockets, IED's, and landmines… I still can't sit through the entire 4th of July fireworks without jumping or getting that tiny panicked feeling that I should probably run for cover. Every explosion, every whistle and BOOM are only a small reminder of the sacrifices made and the true price of freedom.

And while you sit there and enjoy them, while you are in AWE of their power and beauty, I can't help but to sit and think of what each explosion really means… death and destruction. That there are millions of men and women who have given their lives to that same FIRE AND BOOM in the name of our freedom… that there are 48 families from our Battalion who sit and watch with a proud, heavy heart, without their father, their brother, their uncle, their grandfather or son, so that we, some smug and oblivious, can sit here in complete peace of mind, and enjoy our God damned hotdogs and burgers.

The Anxious Mind

We've all seen the Facebook posts, the shares, the articles, and the "Ten Things that Anxious People Do" quick reads. And like me, you probably click on them hoping to find some sort of answers for the crazy shit that you do, like when you pretend that you have plans tonight so that you don't have to walk into the bar by yourself to meet your buddies that you haven't talked to in a few weeks, even though you are completely bored and really, *really* want to go do something.

You click on it and get annoyed at the 3 seconds that it takes to open up.

And then you laugh out loud at how frustrated you get when they make you have to click on that little arrow at the bottom just to go on to the next page.

But you read on anyway. Hoping to learn something new, hoping that the words explain exactly how you feel so that you can stop trying to explain it yourself when everyone gives you shit for how distant you've been lately.

You read every word, careful not to skip an ever-so-important "and" or "because". You catch yourself nodding along with the words, at times, and scrunching up your nose occasionally at how uninspiring the explanation really is.

And ultimately, unfulfilled, you toss your phone back to the mattress and close your eyes for a few minutes to cope with another disappointing article about the strings that control your life.

***

Now, I'm not a doctor, nor did I ever play one on TV, but I can tell you that I have battled Social Anxiety Disorder for as long as I can remember. I can tell you that even at a young age I was unable to perform simple tasks without developing an "oh shit" plan first.

It didn't matter if I was only walking the two hundred yards across the hill to stay the night at my Grandma's, I would still have a stick, a light, and a knife – for whatever creature was lurking beyond the shadows. Or even at during school, where I would sweat through two shirts while trying to outthink the unknown of everyday situations that could possibly happen: *what if she talks to me today, what do I say, what if I trip over my shoe string, what do I talk about with my friends, what if what I say is lame, I forget how to be funny, what do I do to impress her, should I hold her hand, does she want me to kiss her, what if someone tries to rob us on our date, what if there's a fire, a tornado, a blizzard, an accident, what if I get a flat tire, what if... what if... what if.*

Even then, as I planned out all of the safety hazards, escape routes, and ways NOT to get caught while planning our drinking parties... I knew that I was different, I knew that I was special. There were a thousand remarks from my friends, "How did you even think of that?" or "Good thinkin'" and "Dude, stop worrying so much." But they had no idea the lack of control that I had over the things that made my shoulders tense.

***

I suppose that my anxiety was factor in my decision to join the Marines. I was worried that if someone like *me* - who had shot guns since 6 years old, played in the dirt, played army, and was very athletic – didn't sign up for war, then someone who was less qualified would, and that would weigh on my shoulders for eternity.

So I went ahead and joined knowing damn well that it would be tough, but I was completely unprepared for the amount of stress that I would be forced to endure for the rest of my life.

Hey, here's a small piece of advice to those who drag along the weight of an anxiety disorder... don't go into the military, where decisions are made for you and controlling the situation is hardly ever in your hands.

My anxiety was magnified by a 100 times.

Medications didn't help. Counseling didn't help. The VA tried but failed miserably to help.

The course that I was on was full of danger, mystery, and defeat. And traveling that road carrying the dead weight of a tired and anxious mind is debilitating, hell it's downright depleting, to say the least.

But that story is for another time.

All I want to do is to make it more understandable for those who don't live with this cage around their ambitions.

I imagine that it is much like trying to explain to a man what it's like to give birth. Or how you explain war to a person of peace. Shit, it's like trying to describe colors to the blind. It's frustrating, it's exhausting, and it stresses me out to even try to think of the words to reach you.

For me, it's not every second. Hell there's moments of triumph in every day. But the feeling of this invisible force pulling me away from the things that I passionately want to do is certainly blanketing.

It all starts with a thought, *hey, I'm going to go grocery shopping.* And then a sudden strike of fear crashes hard into my throat. My chest tightens. My breathing restricts just a bit, making it feel like I can't take a deep breath, and I before too long I notice that my entire upper body is flexed.

Why?

Well, because a million questions that need immediate solutions rush into my aching head: I wonder who I will see there? Will I have to talk to them? Will I end up saying something stupid? Will I be awkward? Will they laugh at my jokes? What if I know them but forget their name? Do I walk up and say hi to them or let them come say hi to me? What if it's someone that doesn't like me? What about an ex-girlfriend? Or an ex-girlfriend's family member? What if I can't remember why we broke up? Was it on good terms? Bad terms? Am I supposed to be mad at these people? Are they supposed to be mad at me? What if someone talks to me and I don't know what to say?

These are just a few of the questions that constantly play in the background of every decision that I make about everyday life.

And for each question, my mind tries to problem solve and create a plan of action for each scenario... like holly fuck, imagine playing a sport where there are 50 million plays that you have to remember.

See, it's heavy. It's like a pinball machine up here in this balding, glaring, skull. Each problem leads to a new problem to solve, and each idea has a bazillion ways that it could go wrong. My mind wants to solve them all... before I feel comfortable enough to move.

I blame this tactic on the Infantry. **Weigh the risks, make a decision, and adapt when you need to.** But every single decision leads to a thousand other options... and every ounce of my existence is to compute them all to find the best solution.

*Damn it, I'm **still** not explaining it well enough.*

Okay look, do you want to know what it's like to live with high anxiety?

It's sweat. Lots of it. Everywhere. It's sweat stains and soaked armpits all day long. It's sweaty hands and feet, even when you're just hanging with your friends.

It's small tremors in your teeth, in your head, right in your gut.

It's pain. Pain from tense shoulders and neck. Pain from migraines. Pain in your head and eyes. Pain that just randomly develops in your back right before you realize that you are leaning forward, flexed, ready to fight anything that doesn't seem right.

It's the constant questioning of whether or not they got your text, if they're alright, if they're cheating on you, if they were in an accident, or maybe they're ignoring you because you are worthless and they just don't have the nerve to tell you.

It's the staring at your phone while it's ringing, running through all the ways that you could answer and say "hi" but still getting that pit in your stomach at the overbearing task of getting your thumb to swipe across the screen.

It's the desire to get up off the couch and move, but the weights that are dragging you back down. The weights that you drag along with you all day, slowly, inching your way forward one step at a time to all the places that make you happy. Because if you dare went anywhere uncomfortable, it would physically kill you by suffocation

It's the fact that everything that you used to love, now becomes a chore, a job, a constant battle of keeping it together and "trying to relax".

Anxiety is this dome of significantly less oxygen that constantly surrounds you. It traps you. It suffocates you. It changes what is important to you. It forces you to stay at home, to take long naps, to just cuddle up in a hoodie on the couch for the whole fucking day.

It sucks life from you. Pulling and pulling at your stings until you are broken, laying there in a crumbled mess of puppet parts and cord. And then it throws you away into an old box full of all the things that you used to be. And there you sit, stuffed away in the closet, wrapped tightly in the safety of certainty, knowing that this is surely where you will die.

And you slowly become ok with that.

Fifth Chapter
Duty

This Is What We Sacrifice For

This Veterans Day, as I think about and reflect upon the sacrifices made, not just by the brave men and women that I served with, but also, by the long line of courageous and honorable men and women who have kept this country free from the start of our Independence, I can't help but to think about exactly what we were all sacrificing for.

I think, that for some, it was for freedom and liberty; for the safety and well-being of their loved ones back home. And for some, it was to stop evil injustices; to let democracy and choice spread throughout the world. For others, it was for duty and country. (And maybe, just one or two, thought that they'd have a better chance at getting chicks in a uniform??)

But, you see, for me… it was for the way that I was raised, for the way that I was brought up. It was for those values of Love, Family, Freedom, Faith, and Good Moral Character - that were sometimes (and more often than my brothers) beat into my rear end with Dad's homemade yard stick - that I chose and accepted to lay my life down for.

It was for this idea of a Free Nation, where we have the ability to pick and choose our dreams, our goals, and our futures. It was for YOU, and it was for ME… and it was for this idea of US, together, united, one people, under God, who have the strength and the courage to stand up to all things evil and the selflessness to give up their lives to uphold Freedom and Liberty.

You know, I find these same kinds of values, right here, in our small town. Honestly, you don't have to look very far to find friends, family, or even strangers willing to help you out or who will gladly stand up for you. We are a small devoted town, a small collection of diversity, who all share at least one thing in common (no, not Wal-Mart), we are from the hills, the woods, the fields, the villages, the townships, and the communities of Guernsey County. We are all here together.

I often write about the social issues that plaque our society. And, I often poke fun at the trends and fads that seem important now, but will surely fade away over time (like twerking, dear God, I hope that twerking goes away very soon).

But seriously, I would like to take this opportunity to highlight one social issue and lasting trend about our small area that I hope will NEVER fade away; our sense of Community; our value in togetherness, our camaraderie, our hospitality, and our generosity.

It's not hard to find a helping hand around here. Whether you're broke down and stranded alongside some back road, moving in to a new house or apartment, doing home repairs, or in need of a little financial assistance; from benefits to support groups, we have always been there for each other. And, people, that is sacred in an ever-growing self-indulged world.

I can't help but to point out the numerous places around town that are offering free meals, drinks, and other services to our veterans on Veterans Day (and, uhh… if anyone is doing massages or dishes, just let me know). I can't begin to tell you how much that we all appreciate that kind of "thank you" from our community. It goes such a long way to see the support of our friends, neighbors, and fellow members of society. We thank you for that.

From food drives, to donating blankets, hats, and gloves to the needy, to helping the elderly carry groceries, holding open doors, and giving up our seats, we have been lucky enough to come from a close-knit area that still holds manners, respect, and courtesy in high regards.

And I can tell you, right now, that for as long as we hold these values paramount, we will continue to prosper as a society, as a community, and as a nation. We will continue to produce the caliber of men and women who volunteer to sacrifice their life, so that we can have another opportunity to wave at a friendly face in Riesbeck's, to devour another hotdog under the pavilion at Orr's, to huddle together on a carriage ride watching the Courthouse lights, or to buy another deploying buddy one last beer before he leaves at Downtown Arena, Deep Cut, or Steak and Ale.

Small towns like ours… that is what we sacrifice for.

Armed America

Now, before I get into the meat and potadas (yes, potadas), I just want to forewarn any oblivious readers that this may end up being a long, and undoubtedly controversial read. But hey, under the Constitution of the United States, I have the freedom of speech… sooo, I'm gonna use it.

Undeniably, also, under the Constitution of the United States, I am granted (wait, maybe "granted" isn't the right word), I am confirmed the unarguable right to protect myself, my family, my country, and the life of any innocent person, by the ownership and use of firearms. Let me say that again. Our Forefathers thought that the right to protect what you love was so important, that they made it guaranteed under the 2nd Amendment of our Constitution.

Even as I sit here, in my camo shirt (because you have to look the part), I look around my room at my gun rack and gun cabinet (both of which I built myself), and at the NRA certificate for "defending freedom," and the Friends of the NRA coozy that I just got for free at the gun show that I just got home from… and I can't help but think of what my life might have been like if I didn't grow up around firearms.

Well, for starters, I probably wouldn't have felt the need to defend my country and join the United States Marines. I mean, what would've been the point? I, probably, would have thought that firearms were evil and that killing was downright disgusting. Okay, it's just ONE scenario. But, I do want to point out that I don't remember one single Marine in my infantry company that had never fired a gun before. Hell, who knows, maybe there were a couple out of the 180 Marines that I served in Iraq with, but honestly, I do not recall.

I think back to all those mornings rabbit hunting with my dad, brothers, and grandpa while growing up. I think about the responsibility and life values that it taught me: to hunt for my own food, to be able to provide for myself, to be able to protect myself, and to know the power and humbling feeling of taking a life. There's no doubt about it, I had a bit of an ornery streak when I was a kid (understatement). But, through learning the great responsibility of owning, shooting and caring for a deadly weapon, I was, undoubtedly, able to grow up with a profound level of maturity, while understanding so much more about how fragile life is, and how we should live to appreciate and respect it, instead of take it for granted. The value of life, that lesson alone, was instilled into me, more from owning firearms, than from anything else.

So, why do I feel so passionately about being able to own and use firearms? Quite frankly, because I value freedom. And, to be as bold and as frank as I can… the simple truth is, we would not have freedom, if it were not for an armed society.

You say, "bullshit?" Well, you have the right to be wrong. But, I assure you, from the birth of our Revolution, great enemies witnessed the strength of a forming nation that armed its common people; its farmers, merchants, blacksmiths and carpenters; its women, and its children. How would we even have become a free nation if it wasn't for an armed society who stood up to say that they have had enough of the persecution, of evil, and of tyranny?

And I ask you, how is it, that we have stayed a free nation since those very ideas of freedom and liberty were vindicated? Our government? Maybe. But what good is a government if they do not fear their people? What, or who would limit their power? What or who would keep them from becoming the same tyrannical government that we fought to free ourselves from to begin with? The Constitution? Perhaps. The same Constitution that guarantees its people the right of, "A well regulated militia, being necessary to the security of a free state, the right of the people to keep and bear arms, shall not be infringed." Absolutely. You see, the people have been bestowed upon them the right, the responsibility, to keep this nation free. No matter who it is that may threaten it.

Even if our government made us as safe as we could possibly be, no crime, no murder, no threat from an outside source… we would, arguably, still have the need to protect ourselves, our values as a nation, and our life blood… our Constitution, from the threat of a growing, powerful and potentially corrupt government.

The simple truth is, we will only be as free, as we allow ourselves to be.

***

Moving on to a more "individual" approach. Whether or not you want to be, Americans are at war. We all are facing a growing threat of terrorism on the homeland. It is, perhaps, the greatest threat to our safety from a foreign body.

You don't have to agree with me, hell, you don't even have to keep reading if you don't want to. But, as you storm off in a gun-hating, anti-firearm huff and puff of angry curses at my ideologies, pissed off that you just wasted 30 minutes of your Saturday, think about this; as you're heading off to the mall, maybe to watch "The Interview," before it's hacked again, or a theater is blown up, or shot up, and it is no longer "allowed" to be shown to the public… or, hell… maybe you just want to go sit and sip your $5 Colombian coffee as you read your newspaper at some diner in town – but just as you start to read the comic section, 3 angry masked men stand up exposing their rifles, yelling "Allahu Akbar," and start shooting innocent men, women, and children right in front of you.

Of course, you could dial 911 and wait for the police to come save you while people die in a bloody heap right beside you. Hell, you could take your chances and run for it, hoping that they don't notice you shrieking and flailing away. Or, you could hope that somebody like me is sitting next to you, carrying a concealed Glock or M&P. Somebody who is trained and practiced in the use of firearms. Someone who has enough sense to grab your stupid shocked face and pull it down behind the now flipped over table, and tells you to keep your stupid shocked face there while they, and possibly, several other concealed carry permit holders return fire, eliminating the threat and saving dozens of innocent lives.

And, several minutes later, when the cops finally arrive and surround the building, you can run your stupid, flailing ass out there and tell them that you are alive because some regular, common, everyday "Joe," values and exercises his 2nd Amendment right.

But it's up to you, really. Be prepared, or just hope that that day never comes, and assume that the cops will be able to save you before you get executed by a person hell bent on simply killing Americans.

——

I read the news every day, and often while I'm supposed to be doing other things (like working, or cleaning, or paying attention while someone is talking to me). I read the numerous stories of criminals robbing, raping, and murdering innocent people. And, I will tell you this right now… I WILL NOT be one of those innocent, unsuspecting victims! Don't get me wrong, I'm not saying that I will never be robbed or brutally beaten or what-have-you. What I'm saying is… for this very reason, I carry with me a victimless attitude, and with that attitude… a means of protecting myself, the ones I love, the innocent, and yes, even you're stupid, non-logical, anti-firearm, gun hating ass.

Why?

It's simple.

<u>Because, good people will not allow evil to prevail.</u>

I don't know about you, but I can still remember when Cambridge was a peaceful place. A place where you were never woken up by the boom of flashbangs and stun grenades from another drug raid. Or, a place where you didn't have to worry about being stabbed while you were out drinking and having a good time with your friends. I remember back when the front page of our small newspaper used to honor those doing good, not boldly decry another robbery, armed assault, or some meth-lab-drug-raid.

I understand if you became comfortable under the security blanket of a small town. But, listen… it's not the same town as it once was. It's not the same America, as it once was.

People, do not fall victim to this change in society, where for some reason, people feel that they are owed something, and they will stop at nothing to take it away from you. Protect yourselves. Protect your family, not with a mobile phone that can bring you help in "minutes," but with the knowledge and understanding that YOU DON'T HAVE TO BE A VICTIM. Arm yourself with the comfort of realizing that you have the power, and the freedom to protect what you love with a firearm.

Look, my simple point is this… there will ALWAYS be crime and violence; it's a part of our nature. But criminals, and those who wish to do us harm, will not be stopped by laws, or words, or reason… not by locked doors, or security systems, or gun-free zones... they will be stopped by someone like you, who REFUSES to be a victim and understands the true value of a firm, steady, trigger pull.

This Is Not Liberty

Warning: possible political statements and probable political incorrectness ahead

America, the modern day symbol of Freedom, where you are forced to give up a fourth of your income to support programs that give it to those who do not earn it; a place where any citizen can be President, as long as you are a career politician with years of corrupt experience; where criminals hold seats in Congress and create laws that are meant to hold you and me accountable.

America, an Oligarchy enriched by those with deep pockets who buy votes, who buy opinions, and who buy the "facts." It's a place where political corporations own the media and then spin their own political agenda to persuade the public in favor of their own ideas, instead of the transparent truth.

It's a place where racism is taught and hatred is learned.

I, so badly, want to blame it on smart phones and dumb people. But, honestly, it's all of us.

Because here, intelligence is pushed aside for a cute photo of puckered-up lips and a low cut top. Here, sexism, discrimination, and bigotry are justifiable by culture, by region, by religion, and by circumstance. It's a place where we walk on eggshells to not offend a culture for doing what is morally wrong. Here, we are forced to accept all different ideas, views, and opinions... except for our own.

The United States of America... where we are lied to, misled, misguided, oppressed, and controlled by the very same body of government that we created to protect us and our rights.

And, quite frankly, I'm fucking sick and tired of it.

We, The People, are so face deep in our Twitter accounts, our Facebook newsfeed, and Instagram selfies that we don't even care about our lives outside of social media. We couldn't give a shit less about what law was passed to limit our constitutional rights, or what politician was caught breaking what law only to have it simply brushed underneath of the rug, out of view, out of mind, out of existence.

Where is the frustration of the inhumanities that go on every day, right HERE, in our free nation?

Where is the accountability of who WE are, and what America stands for?

Instead, we post a political meme making fun of the way our leadership looks; what utensil they ate with, their hair, what they were wearing. We try to justify hate and racism with "what ifs" and "could have beens." We give up our freedom of knowledge, our right to the truth, so that we can sleep comfortable and clear headed at night, because shit, reality is scary.

People, our values, rights, and freedoms are in jeopardy. Not just by the wicked who are leading this great country, but by the complacency of US, of WE, of the PEOPLE, who care more about how many "likes" we got on a post or a photo than what injustice has happened at the hands of our elected officials and leadership of today.

But how in the hell can we hold them accountable when we don't even hold ourselves accountable? We lie, we cheat, we steal, we bully, we kill, and we corrupt our communities daily. With no regard for what our children and youth see, with no care in the world other than ourselves.

We have gone from a powerful nation with ideas of liberty, justice, and happiness for all, to a country that fusses more about "who wore it better?" than what terrorist organization was created, funded, and supported by our own government.

It's OUR fault, ladies and gentlemen, because we sit back and tolerate it. Because, we accept it. Hell, we even encourage it.

And for that, I am ashamed.

This isn't MY country. *This* isn't what I enlisted and fought for. *These* are not the principles of honor, courage, and commitment that I swore to. This isn't freedom. This is NOT LIBERTY!

Moral men and women of this free country, I beg of you, I implore you... stand tall, be fierce, and give not a grain of ground more in the direction of tolerance.

Because, I fear for us. I fear for freedom. And I fear for the future of United States of America.

Question Everything

I know, how cute. I have created a tag line for some clothing line or sales product aimed at targeting the confused, the impressionable and the disobedient youth.

Well guess what, I *am* talking to you. And all of the other misguided fellows, fellas, and fellinas (girls? I don't know). I'm talking to you <u>all</u>, if you are willing to listen.

Question everything.

No, not for the sake of being an asshole, but because you need to learn how to make your own decisions. Because, if you do not question what is happening, then you accept it. Because, if you do not ask *why?* then you are nothing more than a hammer striking a nail; you will never understand the value of your labor. If you do not search out the answers, then you are part of the problem.

Whoa. Sorry, I jumped into that too quickly. Let me start over.

Who here is familiar with the *Milgram Experiment?* Raise your hand…. no? No one? Okay, let me briefly fill you in.

In a nutshell and paraphrased, Milgram was Psychologist at Yale in the 60's who wanted to determine what made people go along with the atrocities of the Holocaust and why the Germans did not question their orders from authority figures.

Milgram set up an experiment where a volunteer (teacher) would shock a person (learner) for getting an answer wrong in a questionnaire, at increasing levels of voltage, while a "scientist" would keep ordering and encouraging the teacher to continue whenever they hesitated to shock the learner. The learner was part of the experiment and would only act as they were receiving large amounts of electricity by crying out and pleading for the teacher to stop.

What the experiment concluded was that 65% of all teachers continued to the highest level of voltage even with the learner pleading for them not to as the scientist demanded them to continue. It also found that **ALL** participants (teachers) shocked the learner to some level of voltage, simply because they were told to do so. The experiment found that obedience to authority is ingrained into our minds by the way we are raised and brought up.

Shocked?

Well, don't be. Because this experiment was tested again in 2015 and concluded that even a higher percentage of participants would continue to harm people, perceivably to severe levels, simply because they were instructed to do so by someone in a position of power.

What the fuck? Right?

Well, think about it… we are cultivated to follow directions, to be obedient, to do what is ordered, promptly, and without question. We are raised to be doers, not thinkers.

Hell, I remember countless moments of my very own disobedience as a child, jumping up and down on the couch squealing, "I don't care if I get another 'pankin!" (*spanking*, stay with me). Or the angry stomps off into the woods whenever I had had enough of being told what to do and would run away for 33 minutes and 57 seconds at a time.

I remember being conditioned to listen, to follow directions, to do as I am told without question or back talk, or attitude. And God bless my parents, they were just doing as they have learned and felt best to make me succeed in life. But I was taught how to move through this world respecting and following the people who had this power over me.

Hmm, *power over me…* what does that even mean? Your boss? Your parents? Your government? Your God? *Who* has **power over you?**

Jesus, I hope that you all realize that **YOU** have the power over yourself. **You** have the ability to think, to reason, to question, to evaluate, to decide, and to come up with your own decisions, your own path.

I was an Infantry Marine for 6 years. I was told how to walk, where to put my hands, how to dress, what to look like, where to go, what to do, who I could talk to, who I could tell what to do, who tells me what to do, what happens if I do not do it, how fast I have to move, how proficient I have to be, who to fight, when to shoot, who to kill.

I was a number. A pawn. I was piece to the puzzle, and often I didn't know what the picture was. I became nothing; soulless; discouraged; enraged. I was taught that my thoughts did not matter. I was taught that I am only here to follow orders, not to understand, not to decide; just to do.

I've felt the swells inside of me bubble with hate, knowing that I was owned and enslaved by those who had power over me. I can tell you from experience that we are here for something better than that. We are *here* to learn our own way; to become our own keeper.

Shit, we are so submerged in this culture of *do as I say*, that we are teaching our youth not to think for themselves.

Anarchy! Anarchy! Anarchy!

No. That's not what I mean. (Though I reserve my own thoughts on government control, freedom, and liberty.) I do understand that we need guidance, good moral, just, and righteous guidance. We need to know what is right vs. wrong.

But, how do we know what that is? How do we define *right* or *wrong*? We have religion, the Constitution, we have philosophers, psychologists, scientists, and behavioral therapists... but who decides how we *should* act versus how we *want* to act?

Maybe I'm digging too deep here. I don't want you to think that I don't believe in rules. Certainly, we are all governed by rules. Nature has her own; death, age, consequence.

But what we have been given is free will. We have been gifted the ability to think for ourselves. So why the fuck do we still follow in line? Why are we so afraid to ask ***WHY?*** Why are we so ashamed to be different, to walk our own path, to stand out among the masses?

Go to work. Pay your taxes. Don't make noise. Don't raise your hand, save your questions until the end. Don't fight. Don't disturb. Don't blow your whistle. Be on time. Wear this. Don't wear that. Look like him, look like her, look like me. Talk like this. Don't say that. Follow these rules. Follow those rules. Follow <u>my</u> rules.

What has made us stop trying to find an understanding to the things that we are told to do? Why do we feel so powerless to make our own choices?

Question everything.

Sixth Chapter
Vices

Drunk Jake: The Warrior

He's a pretty fun guy, charming even; out there among the laughter and the good times, careless and fearless of reprisals. He's a hero to those who walk this Earth in anxious chains; a true badass in the face of the *cares* and *care-nots*; a renegade, charging headfast into your social gatherings and saying something that'll make you smile.

He's everything that I want to be when I'm around everyone else.

We live in a world full of misdirections and brick walls, a place where we struggle to find who we are without smacking blindly into reasons to change. But do we even want to change? Or should we? Shit, the change inside of me is heavy.

We are the he woeful, so full of worry and panic; overthinking the socks on our feet, the names of familiar faces that we cannot remember, the exit plan for when we run out of words to say. We are the burden of solving problems before they are even problems; the exhaustion of analyzing our surroundings and finding the comfort corners that overlook the room, observing, waiting, hoping that we don't have to talk to people.

This has become my reality. The fear of the social. The haunting task of being like you when I am ME and so much different.

And you know, I've seen it inside of you, as well... the desire to be the things that you are not.

What is this social sting that pricks at you and me? Why do we feel so pushed to fit in? To blend? To mix with the ones who have no fear of judgment?

Hell, I can't stand the thought of you misinterpreting my intentions.

And here I go, back into the dark waters of overthinking every move that I make, living in the heaviness of being wrong. And living with the pain of never knowing, because I didn't try.

So, I like drunk Jake… weekend after weekend, free spirited and fun. Out there talking and nodding about the things that I know nothing about. Shaking hands and smiling, calling him and her by a name that may or may not be right, but not caring because at least I've tried. Going here, going there, making rash decisions and loving it. So free, so alive, so me.

And those of us who walk this path, the ones who bear the weight of caring, we go on living these doubled lives; the one that is carefree and loud, coozy in our hand, singing the wrong words to our new favorite song while holding onto the cutie that we just introduced our self to, laughing and wild, accepting whatever the night might bring….

And then, the one of a pregame pep talk in the mirror, deadlocked on sorry eyes, angry because you cannot leave the house without reminding yourself that you can overcome this anxiety.

Drunk Sex, Alcohol, and Making Love (Drunkly)

As most of you may already know, from either reading previous blog posts or just by knowing me personally, I tend to categorize myself as a strong advocate for making love. And, well, if I'm going to assume that most of you know me well enough to know that I'm a lover (self-appointed) and that you understand my pro-love philosophy on life, then, I should probably, assume that most of you know that I'm, also, a member of the drinking class. (Hell, I've probably drank a few beers with the majority of my blog readers, anyway.) The point is, this has all recently led me to the realization that, all too often, sex and alcohol seem to go hand-in-hand.

See, for me, (if I remember correctly) drunk sex happens something like this...

Well, first off, we more than likely already somewhat know each other (I gave up sex with strangers after the 2nd time I got rid of herpes (p.s. I've never had herpes). So, let's go with scenario number 1... she comes over to my house (which, I spent hours upon hours of thinking about cleaning, and about 10 minutes of actually cleaning). From here, I probably offer her a drink, because I've already had 1 or 2. Then, we probably play poker, or beer pong (my go-to... because in my mind, I'm still 23), or maybe we just chill, drink and laugh the night away. But either way, we drink, we get tipsy, we get drunk... and then, I lead her to my bedroom, I light a candle (because I'm a fucking romantic, and also I need to see exactly what's going on), and then (without getting into the juicy details) we do what drunk, lonely, horny and awesome people do... we get it on 'til the break of dawn... orrrr for 3-5 minutes, whichever comes first.

Now, sadly, it's been a little while since I've made <u>love</u>, but I'm sure that it went something like this...

I spent all day thinking about her, because quite frankly, she's my world. I probably even texted her just to say how much I missed her and told her how I couldn't wait to see her, to hold her, and kiss her. By the time she got to my house, I would already be grilling dinner. I'd pour her a glass of wine, and then, go ahead and top off my glass (sometimes I drink wine when I cook, it's not a big deal people). We'd eat, drink, and mostly just laugh and enjoy spending time together doing whatever... it didn't matter what, because as long as we were doing it together, then it's exactly what I wanted to do. We'd work up a little buzz, hell, maybe even a good drunk, with the passion building the entire time. Then, I'd lead her to my bedroom, light a candle (because I'm a fucking romantic, alright). And then, (again, without getting into the juicy details) we'd do what lover's do, and make love until we were too tired to move... orrr for like 5-7 minutes, whichever came first.

So, I have to wonder... why does it seem that alcohol leads to sex? Now, granted, it doesn't always work that way, but think about it, for those who drink... when was the last time that you had sex/made love without having a drink first? I see it happen a lot (not literally, I mean, I don't literally watch it happen, that would just be weird). But, when I think about it... I see it quite a bit in today's culture. Not only that, but I hear my friends joke about it a good bit. For example, one favorite quote among my circle of friends is something along the lines of this… "we're gonna get so wasted and get it on!"

Now, I've already openly admitted that I'm a drinker (and a good time chaser)… but I still have to question our culture, and our society as a whole… do we NEED alcohol in order to be sexually active? How many of us, who still go out, go out to get drunk and get laid? (You don't have to actually answer that.) But, does it not beg to question the mindset that we have come to acquire when it comes to sex and alcohol?

Okay, I know this doesn't apply to everyone, and really, I'm just working out a curiosity here… but, if we were all to give up alcohol for a whole year, would sexual activity greatly decrease? Better yet, would relationships where both people are drinkers actually benefit from a lack of alcohol, or would they suffer?

Hmm, I don't know people… I don't have all the answers, hell, I'm lucky if I even have any. But, I do know one thing though, when it comes to being "sexy", if it wasn't for alcohol, I'd probably only be 4.7 at best.

30 Days Of Saving Myself (From Myself)

If you know anything about me, then you will know that I am a shameless drinker-inner of the good times and the good booze. Matter of fact, if you creep my facebook page, search the internets for shirtless photos of me, or randomly bombard any social event that I am attending, then you will most likely find me laughing, singing, dancing (or something like it), or tucked away into some corner observing the room, or on my phone, with one hand firmly grasping the coozy covered drink in my hand. It is inevitable. I am a drinker.

The truth is, my social woes and anxiety have plagued me for years… and (without diving too deeply into the "whys" and "why nots") alcohol has been my salvation.

I damn near drink on the daily, yo. And it's pissing me off.

Here's the thing, I have a good personality sober (and not sober), actually… I have a GREAT personality. (Allow me to boast for just a second). I'm a good dude, I'm likeable, I'm charismatic, I make people laugh (sometimes just by looking at me), I can hold a deep conversation, I'm personable, I'm intelligent, and well, I'm (probably) an alcoholic.

Alcohol has been my social crutch for a long, long time. And, even though my blackout-drunk days are very few and way far between, I still drink, almost daily. It might be 1 or 2 drinks a day, or 3-4 (sometimes), to even the ridiculous... a-shit-ton-more-than-I-can-count on the weekends. Yes, I'm a lover of cheap wine, damn near any kind of beer, tequila, liquor, and (in a very manly way) fruity drinks. I just enjoy drinking.

But, it's taking its toll on my health in many more ways than just physically. And it's time to change that.

I've decided to do a "Dry Month" challenge (if that's a thing). I want to go 30 days without having any kind of alcohol. Not just because I need to, but because I want to. I want to get back to being me. And I want to challenge myself in the hardest ways. (Because I'm nuts).

And hey, guess what... I'm bringing you all along with me. I will be posting daily updates (follow along if you like), and maybe, if I feel like it... I will do a "lesson of the week" on why not drinking can be cool, too.

But beware, the language and drama will be real. Enjoy.

(DAILY LOG) 30 Days Of Saving Myself: 30 Days Without Alcohol

This will be my daily log of each sad, lonely, boring, and pathetic day, of me, not consuming, one single sip, of glorious ALCOHOL. Check back daily for each post. Enjoy.

-Day One-

Jan. 2nd, 2016.

Well, I didn't die. I'm not sure if that's because I was still drunk from the Holiday festivities, or if I'm just more of a man than I thought I was. But, hey… that wasn't so bad.

I chose to start this brave endeavor on a Saturday night because, well… because I'm an idiot… or maybe courageous, or perhaps, I just really wanted to test my shit on day one.

Guess what, I drank tea at my buddy's house while we watched football and MMA fights. I was mostly completely sober (if the alcohol was out of my system from the previous night). Hell, I was even funny. I was able to socialize, to communicate, to laugh, to make people laugh, and to be somewhat interesting… without touching one single drop of alcohol.

High five. Gold star. Hell yeah. Smiley fucking face! Go me!

-Day Two-

Jan. 3rd, 2016

Sunday. Funday. Football day. A day that was created for the sole purpose of sipping Mogen David from a red solo cup while moving back and forth from the lazy boy to the couch. But not me. I'm over here slurping Gatorade from a dirty wine glass, faking intoxication and slurred speech to a head-cocked-sideways dog.

What the hell is wrong with me?

Oh yeah, I know... I'm "coping" with the loss of my best friend (for a month).

Stupid football, stupid fanduel, stupid Bengals, stupid Sunday funday.... my head hurts, I need a nap.

-Day Three-

Jan. 4th, 2016

Dear Bold, Strong, Adventurous, Subconscious, Idea-Driven Jake,

I hate your fucking guts.

Who... in the hell... decides to quit drinking the same week that they start a new job??!!

You do, Idea- Jake. You do.

And, if you had a face, I'd seriously consider punching you in it. But you don't have a face, Idea-Jake. You just have ideas… which are all bad, all horrible, all stupid, and all ridiculous.

Why did I let you talk me into this crap? I unfriend you.

Seriously not your friend,

Sober, Conscious, Never-Having-An-Idea-Again Jake

-Day Four-

Jan. 5th, 2016

Today was a crap day for not being able to drink.

My head was thumping more than it has is a long while. I'm not sure if this was due to the information overload at work, or just that my body hates me for not drinking. Either way, today was painful.

Then, I came home from a stressful day at work, only to hear my dirty wine glasses in the sink calling out my name.

"Jake… Jake…. Jacob. Jakester. Jake the snake. J-dawg. J-dizzle. J-man. Juice."

They tried it all. And trust me, it was harder to ignore them than you think.

And, as I opened the fridge for dinner, 2 beers jumped out at my feet, begging me to notice them. Of course, I did. I did notice them. Hell, I even bent down and picked them up, set them on the table beside me and my dinner, as if they were house guests, and told them all about my day.

But they didn't give a shit. Matter of fact, I'm starting to think that they don't care about me all at….

-Day Five-

Jan. 6th, 2016

It's crazy to see how the smallest circumstances can trigger my drinking response.

Something as simple as going over to my brother's house and having dinner… having him ask me what I want to drink as he reaches for the Bud light, and then suddenly remember that I'm going "dry" this month. It's alarming to see how much alcohol has taken over my social skills, that I crave a drink just to sit down at dinner and talk with family.

But, no wonder alcohol is such a crutch; we offer it to friends when they come over, we order it when we go out on dates, we drink it when we socialize at parties or at dinner; we talk about it, we laugh about it, and we tell crazy (semi-acceptable) stories about what we did while we were intoxicated on it.

It's just funny (and a bit frightening) to see how much we actually rely on alcohol, as a culture, to bring us together.

And, since I'm a new found sober person (for 30 days), I hereby declare that we go ahead and look further into this. Standby for more.

-Day Six-

Jan. 7th, 2016

I'm wondering how difficult this would be if I didn't just start a new job. The stress from learning something completely new is just overwhelming. A drink would be spectacular right about now. But, I guess plum pomegranate tea (whatever the hell that is), will have to do tonight.

The headaches are the worst part, right now. I don't know if they are stress related or a-lack-of-alcohol related. Either way, they're pissing me off.

This tea better be potent, 'cause I'm about to get crunk... (or is it crunked???)... I don't know, but here we go.

Here's to all the nights that we remember because we had to drink tea instead of something stronger.

-Day Seven-

Jan. 9th, 2016

If you're ever thinking about hanging out at B-dubs, sober, on a Friday night... DON'T. Matter of fact, I'm not sure if I ever have, before tonight, but I know that I never will again.

Is it a marketing strategy to crank up the noise: the crowd, the TV's, the music; and then stuff the bar packed full of people who want to talk over it all, and run around like wild maniac children???

Because it made me, very badly, want a beer... and about 6 shots.

But hey, I didn't.

Tough night, but I made it.

Screw you , sober B-dubs.

-Day Eight-

Jan. 9th, 2016

Saturday. Time to kick off my heels, let down my hair, and tear shit up.

Well, metaphorically anyway, as I sip on my sweat tea (is there anything else that doesn't have alcohol in it???), and help celebrate my Grandmother's 80th and Aunt's 60th birffdays; packed in tighter than the kitchen sink in my mother's purse (if that's a useful analogy??).

Anyway, we were crammed, stuffed, and elbow to elbow in this tiny seafood restaurant, all 20ish of us; loud, excited, and cackling over one another; I was in need of a celebration drink.

Here's to you guys! (As I raise my glass and throw back the rest of my watered down sweet tea.)

Happy birthday, I love ya, and I'm tired of sweet tea.

-Day Nine-

Jan. 10th, 2016

Well, let's just say that if I was drinking a beer or 2 during that Bengals game, I would have probably smashed my coffee table over my knee. Not because I'm a violent person (because I'm really not, but because I need a new coffee table… and because the Bengals are pathetic, AGAIN, this year.

Moving on.

No drinks, no dranks, no drinky-do's or drinky-dont's. I'm stressed, I'm tired, I'm headached, and even my liver is saying, "Just one, you pussy."

But, I'm gonna hold out.

Just 21 more days.

Son of a bitch….

-Day Ten-

Jan. 11, 2016

Monday's were made for drinking. Especially when you're learning how to be a case manager/activities director for behavioral youth. I don't want a drink… I need a drink.

And sleep. And a massage.

Actually, I think I'll just trade all of that in, and settle for that billion dollar lottery ticket.

Go ahead and send me that oversized check, I've already cleared a spot on the wall above my sofa. Thanks.

-Day Eleven-

Jan. 12th, 2016

I stopped being able to form words and sentences. I'm not sure if this is a common side-effect from not drinking for 11 days, or if this is what happens when you work as a case manager in a youth residential treatment facility.

The truth is, I have no idea if a drink would help me, hurt me, or give me a bigger headache than I already have.

I still think about drinking a lot, but I also think about going to bed... at 8:30pm.

Good night.

-Day Twelve-

Jan. 13th 2016

I came crawling through the door like some living dead zombie tweaking for some fresh brains and blood.

My blood was in the bottom crisper drawer of the fridge, begging me to pop a top.

But I was able to make it to the sofa, where I stared at a blank tv screen for however many minutes it took for me to realize that I was home… and alive.

If alcohol doesn't kill me, then my new job will.

I need a new hobby to abuse for the next 18 days. I wonder how addictive bird watching can be??

Anyone?

-Day Thirteen-

Jan. 14th, 2016

I don't want to admit that I went to bed at 8:30… so let's just say that I fell asleep "early." I was so exhausted that the thought of a drink only drifted through my mind for a few flashing moments. To be honest, all I could really think about was going to bed.

Sooo, basically, I have this whole thing figured out now: work until you are completely and utterly mentally drained and void of any reasonable thought, and then just go to bed "early."

Piece. Of. Cake.

-Day Fourteen-

Jan. 15th, 2016

Poker night with the guys.

I walk in to the smell of fermented air and busted ass, I'm carrying a coozy covered bottle of water.

Commence 10 minutes of sissy jokes.

End jokes. Begin Explanation.

Begin another 10 min session of sissy jokes.

Give up explaining something that men drinking beer wouldn't understand.

Suddenly become comfortable with not drinking.

Play poker. Lose poker. Stay Sober. Still have fun.

That's… a fucking win!

-Day Fifteen-

Jan. 16th, 2016

Against my better judgment, I adventured back to B-dubs with the guys to catch the game.

I'm not sure if I've grown up this much in the last week or if I'm just not as irritable, now, but it really wasn't that bad. My sweet tea was sweet, my wings were perfect, and the atmosphere was a little less hostile.

I found it sort of ironic (and funny) that my dudes ordered "my wing beer," Blue Moon… even though they used to question my manhood about it back in my "drinking days," (ok, so like… 2 weeks ago).

And I didn't even hesitate explaining why I'm not drinking when they questioned my bizarre behavior.

"Are you sick?"

"Are you dying?"

"Has your body been taken over by aliens?"

No guys, I'm just not drinking, for me, because I NEED to do this, because I WANT to do this, because, if not, then I'll never know how to handle my problems like an adult, like a man, like a mature, reasonable, rational, sane, nonalcoholic, alien person.

Besides, I had fun, anyway.

-Day Sixteen-

Jan. 17th, 2016

Is it just me, or did God invent beer and football so that they could go hand-in-hand together? I'm pretty sure that He did, because that just makes sense.

It would have been nice to watch the playoffs with a nice cold brew. But, honestly… I hardly even thought about it. Hell, I don't even know if I DID think about it!

How crazy it is, to see just how much I don't think about alcohol, a mere 2 weeks after my last sip for 30 days.

I'd pat myself on the back, but my arms are too short….

-Day Seventeen-

Jan. 18th, 2016

The habit of drinking is slowly starting to slip away.

My first thought, when I went to grab a beverage for dinner, was water. And I alllmooost completely ignored the fridge full of alcohol when I opened the door to grab that bottle of H2 izzo.

I guess what I'm trying to say is, after 2 weeks, I'm a pro. (Ok... ok... semi-pro? Minor leagues? Single A minor leagues?)

Alright, basically, I'm the bat boy.

But at least I'm in the dugout!!

-Day Eighteen-

Jan. 19th, 2016

Today was the first day that I actually realized that I didn't want, or even think about an alcoholic drink.

I came home from another stressful day, and instead of thinking about a drink, I thought about working out and re-hydrating for, yet, another sweaty-stressful day at work.

Not to mention that we went out to eat for my brother's birthday and I ordered a water with TWO lemons!

Who the hell am I??!! What I have done to myself??!!

Next thing you know, I'll be going vegetarian and doing yoga in my cheetah-print spandex....

(But, that'll be next month's blog)

-Day Nineteen-

Jan. 20th, 2016

So, I can come home from a stressful day and not have a drink. I can cook, and not have a drink. I can watch a movie, football, or Teen Mom and not have a drink... weeelllll, ok, if I ever watched Teen Mom then I would probably need a drink.

But my routine is changing. I can see it as clear as day.

I'm feeling like a brand new man.

And I'm getting taller. (not really)

-Day Twenty-

Jan. 21st, 2016

I will be completely honest. I thought about alcohol 3 times today. All of which were jokes. And all of which were made WITHOUT even wanting a drink.

That says a lot.

Now, don't get me wrong, the jokes weren't even funny.

But at least I was able to think about alcohol without wanting to actually drink it.

Boom.

-Day Twenty-One-

Jan. 22nd, 2016

Everyone is out in a panic grabbing up food and wine in anticipation of this winter storm, and I'm over here picking up pizza and bottles of green tea. Lord knows what would happen if I was stuck in the house for 24 hours drinking nothing but water and eating canned soup.

But here's the thing, the thought didn't even cross my mind, to go and grab alcohol, or that I needed, or even wanted a drink.

But the pizza… yeah, I would've drove the 4-wheeler through a blizzard to go get that.

Priorities, people... Priorities.

-Day Twenty-Two-

Jan. 23rd, 2016

Let's just say that I managed to make it through another Saturday night without drinking.

Oh. And I won $370 in a poker tournament.

I celebrated with ice cold water and a movie.

Score.

-Day Twenty-Three-

Jan. 24th, 2016

7 days left. That's, pretty much, like a week.

Which works out just fine, because I'm sort of overdue on a celebratory drink.

Football is so much more serious when you can have a beer.

Eww.

-Day Twenty-Four-

Jan. 25th, 2016

What is this, Monday. It feels like a Monday. Monday's are a pain in my ass. Today was a pain in my ass. Today, would've been a good day to drink.

Instead, I came home, worked out, rented a movie and went to bed.

I'm starting to think that sober people don't know how to have much fun.

-Day Twenty-Five-

Jan. 26th, 2016

What. The. Hell.

Two Mondays in a row?? How is this possible?!

Today was even worse than yesterday, on the stressed and shitty scale.

It won't be the alcohol that kills me, it'll be this job.

Also, I had a dream about a tall Blue Moon, and then another one, and then just one more for good measure.

I miss Blue Moon. I miss drinking.

But, to be honest… I really don't think about it all that much during the day. My mind is too far gone to even have the mental space for just one more thought.

I guess that's why Subconscious Jake was trying to remind me about my long lost buddy, Mr. Blue Moon.

-Day Twenty-Six-

Jan. 27th, 2016

I decided that alcohol isn't the answer.

Instead, I will punish my body with snack food and multiple workouts.

This is, obviously, the answer.

Don't argue with me.

-Day Twenty-Seven-

Jan. 28th, 2016

The plan is to get up early, workout, go to work, question my stupidity, come home from work, sweat out all of the stress, shower, go to bed at the same time that my grandparents would, and then wake up and repeat.

I'll be looking like Magic Mike in no time at all.

-Day Twenty-Eight-

Jan. 29th, 2016

Fuck you, Channing Tatum.

Magic Mike??

More like, Jacob the Jester.

Either way, pizza, junk food, 3rd helpings, 4 squeezes of Mio Energy drink enhancer, and poker with the guys.

(Yes, I have a coozy on my water bottle.)

-Day Twenty-Nine-

Jan. 30th, 2016

Well, tomorrow is day 30. But today is a Saturday. I should be out raising hell until the break of dawn with all the rest of the (almost) 31 year olds.

Wait, what?! 31 year olds don't do that kinda shit anymore?

Are you sure??

Son of a bitch.

So going to a movie by myself, and staying in and working on writing things was the "correct" thing to do??!

That was normal??

What the hell?!

This whole not drinking thing is really starting to fuck me up.

-Day THIRY BITCHEZZZ-

Jan. 31st, 2016

The day that will go down in infamy. Or not.

But it IS the last day that my liver and I will be best friends.

Although, this whole experience has honestly shown me that I don't HAVE to drink… that I don't NEED to drink.

So with that in mind, if I drink tomorrow, it will be because I WANT to, not because I NEED to.

But here's the thing… I was really starting to enjoy tea….

Lessons From Week One Of Sobriety: Idiot.

Well, week one of not drinking is over with. Am I a new man? Hardly. But, there are a few things that this week of excruciating sobriety has taught me.

#1.   Stress is my trigger. Which I pretty much already knew. But to sit back and watch it from a "not giving in" kind of perspective is, to say the least, eye opening. I mean, I already know about my anxiety and other issues related to being uncomfortable socially… but when you always give in, you know that you have a way (an unhealthy way) to cope.

But now, not allowing myself to reach for that coping mechanism has shown me that I'm, pretty much, an idiot… well, ok, kind of. In reality, it's made me have to deal with this stress and anxiety in other ways. Like imagining people naked. Wait. No. That's only for when I'm publicly speaking, right? I don't know, but I'll figure it out.

#2.   Restaurants need more drinks that are healthy for you. I'm tired of water, I'm getting tired of tea, and I don't drink pop (we call it pop 'round these parts).

So what options are out there? If I'm trying to stay away from something that is unhealthy for me, then I sure as shit don't want to drink something that is loaded with sugar, or carbs, or calories, or whatever else that makes my teeth rot and pants too small. What do sober people drink?????

#3.   This is hard, but do-able. Obviously, this is difficult. While I'm not the type to get shitfaced every time I have a drink, I am the type that likes to drink a couple of drinks with anything that I do. (Except working out. Alcohol and workouts are a horrible mix. Just... trust me.)

So, yes, this is bullshit. I don't enjoy it. And I want to quit.

But, I'm not going to. Because that is exactly why I'm doing this – to prove that I can – to be faced with a challenge and overcome it.

Oh, and to fit into last year's jeans.

Lessons From Four Weeks of Sobriety: Who Am I?

Alcohol? What is *Alcohol?*

I mean, I'm quite familiar with iced water with 2 lemon slices, or two refills on my sweet tea; but alcohol… I forget what that's like.

I see people laughing and cheersing, clinging those brown long neck bottles in a ceremonious celebration of good times, while I'm over here trying to start up conversations about my 401k: This is the *new* me, the *responsible* me, the *I-almost-tucked-my-shirt-in-before-I-left-the-house* me.

I think I'll start a family, maybe buy a little house in the suburbs, you know, one with red shutters and a white picket fence. I'll have backyard BBQ's and trivia night with my mature friends, sipping on fresh made lemonade and snacking on multigrain crackers and lettuce leaves, *or something.*

I think I will start investing money into businesses with names that I cannot pronounce correctly, like: *GIVENCHY, STELLA ARTOIS,* and *BVLGARI.* I'm going to be a sophisticated sober person.

Well… not exactly.

You see, in a month of going sober I learned 2 things.

#1. I sure as shit can go without alcohol if I chose to.

And #2. I really like drinking.

Yes, it was difficult in the first two weeks to be around my friends and family, to come home from a stressful day at work, to go out on the weekend and not have a single sip of that courage in a can. Hell, I thought it would kill me.

But, I made it. I talked to people without a drink in my hand. I relaxed at night without a glass of wine or cold beer. I even laughed and *almost* danced without any shots at all. I proved that I am capable, and that is a powerful fucking feeling.

But, you know what? **I like drinking.** I enjoy that little gitty feeling of caring a little less about doing everything right and just living in, and enjoying the moment. I enjoy the comfort of a coozy covered can squeezed gently in my hand, held at chest level, while I'm talking about girls, or guns, or the crazy shit that we go into last weekend with my friends.

I'm not ashamed of who I am, of where I come from, or what I do. Every day I work on the man that I want to be. And this month long challenge to put down the adult beverages, has taught me that I'm *okay* with being the man that I am.

And if you can feel that… then raise up a cold one, and toast with me to the things that we cannot change, and to those that we just simply don't want to. Cheers.

Seventh Chapter
Determination

Risky Business

There's an old Proverb that says, "He who stands closest to the edge, has the best view."

Think about that for a second… let it sink in. See yourself inching closer to the edge of some cliff or canyon, knowing full well of the danger of falling, but being rewarded for your courage with the breath-taking view of some majestic valley river or painted canyon walls.

Okay, now think about this, I completely just made that Proverb up (but, if you'd like to put that down in some book of Proverbs, go right ahead. Just send the royalty check to my mother, because, Lord knows that I still owe her for the loss of her sanity from the shenanigans of my youth) ((Sorry, Maw)).

Anyway, that's the long way of saying this… that with great risks, come great rewards, orrr, well, great failures. But, I'm pretty certain that this is what life is all about: testing your boundaries, pushing through your comfort zones, and betting on yourself.

About a year and a half ago, I did just that. I quit my long tenure of working for my father, who has managed to build his small construction and excavating company into a well-known and prosperous one; one that I (and my brothers, friends, and family) have helped him build over the years, as well. I can still remember several old houses, roofs, and pads that I helped him build (well, ok, that I helped get in the way of him building). But seriously, I have worked for my father for as long as I could swing a hammer or push a shovel.

But, there came a point in my life when I wanted to do more, to be more, to aspire to more than just what my father had started. I wanted to be my own person, to set out on my own path, to create my own destiny. So, in other words, basically, I just wanted a year off from work, and so I quit.

I passed up on a good paying job, with good, easy-to-work-with company (and good exercise) because I wanted to do my own thing: I wanted to write.

After-all, I did spend $55,000 on an English degree, and let's be honest, you don't even have to speak English to push a shovel.

So, I told him that it was time to move on. And move on, I did, for the most part, like... I moved on to sleeping in til 10am, and then, I moved on to searching for jobs for 2-3 hours a day. I tried to sell a movie that I wrote (it didn't work) and then, I moved on to almost giving up, to almost saying *F-it I'll just rob banks for a living or something...* and then... well, then, I started writing, again. It seems that I excel the most when I back myself into a corner, blindfolded, hands tied, and dizzy from self-inflicted circles. In other words, I do my best work when I have nothing else left to hold on to, but hope.

Since saying good-bye to almost having shares in the company stock, to the comfort of knowing what's ahead... since then, I have freed myself from the chains of complacency and opened up my heart to following a dream: to be a writer. I started a blog (that's what you're reading right meow) and then, just like that, I started a very inspiring book about my grandfather (and hopefully, that's what you'll be reading sometime soon).

Without taking that risk, without letting go of what was easy, then I would never have forced myself up from the mundane and into a fresh breath of excitement and optimism that I am currently inhaling in gulps. I couldn't be more enthusiastic about the book, which is not too far from being finished, and about the success of this blog (that I only started because I missed writing). And, really, it all came about just from taking that leap.

No, it won't ALWAYS work out... but, taking chances IS a good thing... (unless it's with birth control or firearms). No one else is going to chase your dreams for you. It's something that YOU have to decide to do. And, it's probably going to be scary as hell, too. But, without taking any risk… you're not living, you're just breathing.

So, I guess what I'm saying is, go ahead and inch closer to that edge… because even if you fall, sometimes, the view is the best on the way down.

A Writer?! What The Hell Is Wrong With You??!

Huhhh??

Yeah, that seems to be the leading look that I've been getting lately, when I spread around the word that I'm going to be a writer. That I no longer want to be a SLAVE to the Corporate America. And that judgmental look is often followed by invasive questions and less-than-satisfying job ideas that are, pretty much, no less than code for, "Dude, what the hell is wrong with you? Are you F-ing crazy?!"

Well, to answer your questions, quite bluntly, the voices in my head say, FUCK OFF.

But, hell, I guess I'd be a liar if I said that I haven't, on occasion, caught my weaker self giving me the same damn look just before I flick out the light and tuck my over-thinking, life-pondering ass into bed.

So, why do I want to be a writer?!

Well, to be honest, I'm not sure if writers actually want to be writers in the first place. As far as I know, it's something that we NEED to be. (OKAY, Yeah, I know... that's a laughable and debatable statement.)

But look, in the most simplest of terms, we just don't see the world in the same light that you do. Where you see blue, we see lazy summer days at the lake, laughing and drinking with friends; and, where you see red, we see those exotic sunsets, side by side, hand in hand with the person that we love.

We are visionaries, challengers of the norms, the pushers of limits; warrior poets, where our pens are our swords and our voices are arrows. We are honorable, noble, struggling peasants of our own deep thoughts.

And, I assure you, that it doesn't make much sense to us either. Where it comes from... Hell, I couldn't tell ya. I just remember the first time that it flowed through me, pumping out words in ink, like blood, splattering thoughts from the deepest veins of my soul; I was nearly 12. And, I had no idea what I was doing, playing with the visions in my head, vomiting insight and enlightenment until I was empty, weak, and tired. I had no idea where it came from, nor do I even know, now, where it comes from... I just know that it HAS to come out.

All I've ever wanted to do was inspire people. To make them feel, tingle, smile, laugh, cry, reflect, and grow. And it's hardly an easy task. Actually, it's damn exhausting, it's frustrating, and strenuous.

I fear that even my own mother (though my biggest fan) still has no idea the labor that writing involves. Even now, as I stand at my computer (because I pace back and forth when I write), my head is heavy, aching with thought; my eyes burn from reading, and from not blinking, until I pause and pull away from the screen; my shoulders are tense with revelation; and, I have to remind myself to breathe and breathe deeply.

But, the most difficult part (in my opinion) is not being able to find the words when you have so much to say. Writer's Block, as they call it… will, one day, be the death of me… or my walls, or my chairs, or my pens, or whatever other unfortunate hard object that restitutes my fit of rage (oh shit, I AM crazy!)

I suppose, when I step back and take it all in, when I look at what it takes to be a writer, how easily it is to fail, how hard it can be to make a living at it… I guess I can see your cause for concern.

But, just as a nurse is invested, full heartedly, in what they do; writers are as devoted, too. Just as a firefighter needs fire to feel relevant; we too, need to dance among the flames. And, as a gambler understands that you cannot win if you do not risk; writers are willing to go all-in.

Why be a Writer, you ask??? Well, it's because it's who I am….

Bumpy Roads

Bumpy roads will lead you home.

Well, in my case, anyway, it usually leads to me picking up all the loose change that ended up popping out of the center console from my inability to give a damn on back roads.

For some reason, the freedom of those country roads make me wanna go fast, just like Ricky Bobby — alright, go ahead, I know you're already thinking it, "if you're not first, you're last". Matter of fact, in my part of Ohio, damn near every road is bumpy, long and hard; and in one way or another, literally, it leads you back home. And, if you live here, then you probably assume that that's just how new roads are made — with potholes already in them.

So, there you are cruising down Main Street Ohio, or rounding some tree-lined-trash-in-the-ditch-bend on some country road, while those potholes have you headbanging like a die-hard Zeppelin fan, spilling your white-chocolate-caramel-mocha-latte-iced-frappuccino (or beer, whichever), and "trying" to sing all the right words to Chris LeDoux's Life is a Highway.

Soon, you to realize that you need to be dodging them sumbitches before you become concussed. Next thing you know, you're swerving like Aunt Judy on a 2-for-1 margarita night. And, in which case, you're probably taking them back roads home, anyway.

And, again, Bumpy roads will lead you home.

But, you see, I'm not really talking about those kind of roads; I'm reaching a little deeper than that. I'm talking about those rugged roads of life that jar you so hard, that you have to pull over and revaluate which direction that you really want to go. I'm talking about the roads that you end up lost on, out in the middle of nowhere, desperate, alone, and scared; the roads that don't ever show up on that map of life that you've been following.

These are the hard roads. The toll roads. The roads where we all pay our dues. And let me tell ya, you <u>will</u> pay your dues.

But, let me tell you right now, we need these roads. Hell, we even need the flat tires, the broken axels, the bent frames, the busted break lines, and all of those electrical problems that come along with them (metaphorically, of course). Because, this is where we fix ourselves… pulled over alongside these nearly impassable pathways.

This is where we redirect our compass, and point it towards home, towards salvation, towards resurrection.

I can tell you, right now, that I am thankful for the rocky roads, the potholes, the steep hills, and the sharp bends of my life. Hell, I've never been to more beautiful places, than to where these bumpy roads have led me. Bouncing, banging, swerving, and turning myself around, is how I've discovered who I am and what it takes to get me to where I want to go. It's these ass-kicking roads of life that have instilled in me the ability to change, to adapt to adversity and to pull my battered and beaten self out of deepest of ditches on life's bumpy roads.

After all, where I come from, smooth roads don't lead you to beautiful places... it's the hard roads that will take you there.

Surviving The Fall

Look, we've all been there... laying on our backs in a mangled, twisted mess, looking up at the cloudy grey skies in devastation, with desperation, and wondering "how in the hell did I end up here?"

"How did I let myself get so low; get so far off track? At what point did I lose sight of who I am and what I want? And for God's sake, how do I pick myself up off of my bruised and battered ass, and carry on?"

Yeah, we've all been there… and if you deny it, then let me remedy your denial with a backhand to the face.

The Fall.
It's funny how we never see it coming, how we never see that stumbling block until we're lying next to it, on its level, just as low and as hard and just as much an obstacle to ourselves as whatever it was that put us there in the first place. It gives new meaning to the words "too late," as we struggle to realize that we are already drowning.

You see, at this point, we have already failed. We have already allowed ourselves to succumb to whatever hardship, whatever turmoil, whatever travesty we have encountered. And, to be quite honest, we simply became our own enemy. We failed to remember the last time that we were here; the last time that we were broken, and yet, we healed. We failed to see the true value that we possess; the kindness, the compassion, the ability to help others, to help ourselves, the strength of love and hope…

But, damn… here you are again, beat down by the blows of life… swollen… red… and ready to give in, to give up….

If you were ever looking for that defining moment… THIS IS IT!

This is where you make your stand.

But, I'm not going to tell you to stand up and brush yourself off… No, that's bullshit. That's something people say after they forget what it was like to ever be that low.

You see, sometimes, you just can't get back up. Sometimes, you have to fight from your back; and even then, you're forced to claw and scratch and bite your way back to your broken knees, just so that you can jab and punch and gouge your way to your limping feet. Hell, sometimes, it's not about standing back up at all… it's just about surviving.

I'll admit that I'm a self-tripper (no, not the psychedelic kind, although, I do, occasionally, see neon sound waves after too much coffee). I simply mean, that I tend to get into my own way. I am my greatest obstacle. But even when things seem as low as they can get; even after sabotaging my own success, after taking up arms against my own sanity, even after becoming my own worst enemy… there is no greater ally to myself, than, myself.

What I mean is, if you want to survive the fall, you have to start by helping yourself. Life is ebbs and flows. It is waves of highs and lows. This isn't some soft pond tucked neatly and calmly into the rolling hills of Mother Nature's farm, no… we are stranded on some beautiful glimmering ocean that does all it can to push and pull us under.

Yes, there will be calm days, but there will also be rough seas. And when you're rattled from whatever flotation device that you're in and you fall, and you plunge into those cold, sharp waters… just remember to take a deep breath… to float, and swim, and float, and swim… until you see land, and then kick like hell… and hope for a nude beach.

Why Do I Do It?

I'm cruising down some back road, mid-July, with the windows down, the country music loud (probably too loud), watching the stars and the dust fly up in the red glow of the one good taillight of my old blazer; I'm 16 years old and just out driving around because I can. My Garth Brooks Double Live CD goes silent, and then those red hot fiddles of "Ain't Going Down Til The Sun Comes Up" rev up and squeal powerful from the 2 still working speakers that I have left. The excitement sends chills down my arms as I struggle to scream out all the wrong words just as fast as Garth does the right ones.

I blow through a stop sign and sling gravel wide around a blind turn, and almost end up in an empty beer can ditch… but I've never felt more alive, I've never felt more free.

Looking up at the it's-past-my-curfew-sky, gazing out at the look-at-me-I'm-free stars glittering just like the dust floating in my head lights, it hits me… that flash of fire in the deepest pits of my soul, that jolt of life coursing through my veins, that shimmer of insight building up in my head, as the word FREEDOM forms on my tongue.

I pull over, grab the notepad wedged between my seat and center console, and just like that the words come pouring out... (sort of like those beers that mom had found hidden in my room). Twenty minutes later, I'm drained, empty of thought, and yet, so inspired and burning with life. But, right there, in that notepad, I have another poem that I will rush home to read to my scolding mother.

*****

Why do I write? And why do I feel the need to share?

Well, I really have to think hard about it, because at this point, it's so much a part of me, that it's just as natural as kissing the people that you love (with tongue, but not too much tongue... kinda-like, half tongue). But you get the point, it's intimate; and just as naturally so.

In the beginning, I wrote for me. I wrote because the world didn't make sense to me, and because I had so many questions and ideas and thoughts that, ultimately, formed into words and those words turned into poems and those poems turned into me. And therefore, I was able to discover who I am, and faintly, what this world is.

As I started writing, I started growing… I started giving life to those feelings and ideas. I'm not sure how to explain it better than describing it as an institution for myself, where I was the teacher and I was the student. With each new poem, I was learning more about myself, more about this life, than what I would actually learn in school.

Matter of fact, I wrote more during class time than I did on my free time. All it took was a simple idea, a small spurt of inspiration, and off into my own little world I would go, off into the back pages of my notebook, where I would scribble out pieces of my heart and soul in order to better understand exactly who I am.

Ever since the beginning, I had the need to share. And my poor loving mother was my audience, and after each new poem, I would run to her and read it proudly (and then watch her face crinkle, wondering what the hell I just said). But she was my biggest fan, and my first fan, and she was my support, and even if she didn't care for the poem itself, she still pretended to find it interesting (God bless her heart).

But the thing is, back then, I didn't need for her to understand it, I just needed her to hear it, I just needed to share it.

*****

So why do I need to share?

Honesty, I think it's just who I am. I've always been open and honest and able to bare my soul with no regrets. I think that it's an intimacy thing. No, not like 50 Shades of Grey intimacy, I mean like the hopeless romantic kind. I mean, the big heart, caring for people, compassion, bonding (not bondage), and connection kind of intimacy. I think I just want to give myself to others.

For instance, for the longest time I would read all of my old (semi-decent) poetry to my girlfriends. Not to show off my talents or to try to impress them, it wasn't anything like that at all. It was about baring my soul, undressing my heart, my wounds, and stripping my most inner self naked in front of her... so that she could see me for who I am, so that she could know my pains, my doubts, my troubles, my weaknesses, and my desires.

*****

Now, when I write today, I write because I want to inspire, not just me, but others. I want, so badly, to open up their minds to a new idea that they might not have reached if it wasn't for the words that I wrote down. I want to make people feel, laugh, cry, smile, and dig deep in self-reflection of who they are and where they stand in life. Because, honestly, are we not here to discover who we are? Are we not here to learn as much as we can about us and this world we live in? Are we not here for each other?

And I share because, well, I want you to know who I am. I want you to know that you are not alone if you feel the same way that I do. I want you to know that hurdles can be broken, that obstacles can be overcome, and that wounds can heal... that honesty, love, compassion, and faith can still lead you to everything that you will ever need.

I share because these words, these *ideas*, need an audience... because, they need YOU in order to come alive.

Eighth Chapter
Family

Where We Come From

This time of year always gets to me.

I remember mother's "countdown to Christmas" calendar where we would peel open one window for each day. And literally, the first thing in the morning, running barefoot to the kitchen in nothing but my tighty-whities, peeling open that window counting down 22, 21, 20 days 'til Christmas, while the Christmas music from mom's miniature winter village filled the dining room with Christmas spirit.

It was the anxiousness of waking up every hour on Christmas Eve night to check and see if I was good enough for Santa to make it to my house yet. But, also, being too nervous to open the door, walk down the hallway and look. So, I would just lay in bed and listen, hoping to hear him stacking the presents underneath of our tree.

It's the holiday traditions of family gatherings: food, laughter, cards, toys, BB guns, and new ways to mix an alcoholic drink, (and for a few awesome years, going out drinking to the Hi-Li with the cousins Christmas night... after all, they ARE open 365 days a year.)

There has always been so much love and support filling our stockings and hearts this time of year, when it's coldest, and when we need that warmth the most.

Now, as I grow older (and stay out waayy earlier), I find myself wanting to hold onto that, to spread that, to cherish that, and to recognize that *love* as much as I possibly can.

But, to be completely broke and honest... I haven't had the money over the years to spoil those that I love as much as they deserve.

And during all of those dollar menu and re-gifting years, I have learned that love does not come from your bank account; it comes from your heart.

It comes from those memories of Crown Royal
Euchre tournaments with Uncle Matt, Aunt Patti and
the cousins. It comes from the homemade cookies,
haluski, and mixed drinks that mom spent hours
making. It comes from the hustle and bustle of a
spread-out family who will do everything in their
power to make it to YOUR Christmas celebration, on
top of the other 6 that they had planned that day.

And so, being the broke ass, scarcely-semi-talented
writer that I am, I took it upon myself to capture who
we are and where we come from in a poem just about
that.

I've had several requests to read this poem, already.
So Ladies and Gentlemen, without further ado, it is
my stressful pleasure to give to you, Where We Come
From.

Where We Come From

Mostly empty Old Milwaukee cans, stashed
behind the wd40 and lined quarts of oil,
clamor from this year's litter of curious
Calico kittens; and there's new stubborn

Slovak blood rolling down the old stains on
Grandpa's greasy knuckles. But he just
grunts like the buck at the backyard apple
tree, where he built cousin Ju-Ju's square

plywood tree fort that now gives shelter to a
lost nerf football and a few forgotten GI-
JOE army men; there was a time, back
before he had us grandkids searching

faithfully for "purple-assed-buzzards," that
he would have cursed at the pain of a
slipped wrench on a buddy's rusted old
Chevy, back when the pain of hard labor

could still make new scars, like the blizzard
of '77 when the water pipes froze solid and
he lumbered out into the wind and fury, both
before and after work, to stretch a garden

hose across the driveway in order for his
little girls to take a cold shower. Or, back
when Grandma's open heart would carry in
another stray animal, or another friend

without a place to go, back when the guest
bedroom was always full, and no mouth
would go unfed, unless it was hers or his; a
cursing time, but a blessing time; when he

taught little girls to feed the horses,
peacocks, and chickens before school, so
that they could run off to class learning how

to live with the shit on their shoes; or how to

get dirt and blisters on their hands, shoveling
out the chicken coop into five gallon buckets
to fertilize the sweet peas and cabbage; or
plucking bloody feathers from a freshly axed

hen for dinner, and standing on a bucket at
the sink in the garage washing out the
gizzards; or thumbing off dried shit from
those brown speckled eggs with a grease

bubbled bar of Irish Springs soap, eggs that
were gathered on the ice or in the mud, both
morning and night. Then, sending them off
to church, neighbors, or school, in saved

cartons to those who needed them more than
a house of half full stomachs. "There is
always someone less fortunate than you," I
remember Grandma would often remind us,

while ignoring another one of my temper
tantrums on the floor of Kroger's candy
aisle as we filled church Christmas baskets;
or then, when she had to cash in her silver

certificates in order to buy Pamra's braces.
But now, here in the garage, Grandpa's new
greasy bubbles on the same green bar of
soap turn my small, dirty-fingernailed hands

grey while I watch him wipe that still

stubborn, Slovak blood dry on Aunt Penny's
new birthday flannel. And the dogs are
barking at mom walking across the hill,

while Grandma is sweeping leaves from the
chairs and swing on the patio, as more
familiar faces sling gravel up the drive; their
hatches filled with homemade pie, pagachi,

and corn on the cob for the fire. The cousins
are dressed too nicely; and later, we will be
scolded for our creek soaked shoes and grass
stained jeans, swinging at lightning bugs

with sticks, and bragging about sleeping in
the tent all night, but waking up, instead, at
the foot of Grandpa's snoring bed in Aunt
Patti's old basketball sweats.

Ode To My Mother

Well, it's that one day a year, again, where we tell our
mothers just how much we appreciate them (LISTEN
you better not be shaking your head in agreement,
right now, you should be telling your mother how
much you appreciate her every chance you get!)

But anyway, public service announcement aside, I
just wanted to give my own Maw a little shout out,
"Hey Maw! Look, I'm on the internets!!"

Okay, but seriously, thank you, mother for always putting up with my shit. And, at times, cleaning up my shit. You're the Best!!

So Maw, here's a cute, silly, stupid, little poem that I wrote just for you.

Ode To My Mother (Because I Don't Wanna Get Grounded, Again)

Mother,
You brought me into this world,
and have threatened to take me out of it.
(P.S. I'm really glad that you didn't.)

You've kissed me "hello," "goodbye," and
"it'll be alright." You've said that you love me
more times than I have ever told you. And you've
also shown me, by forgiving me, (and still admitting,
in public, that I'm yours).

I've made you yell at me more times than you've
ever wanted to. So much so, that even when my
brothers
did something wrong (which you never thought
possible),
"Jacob Paul!" were the first words that came from
your
scolding lips.

The same lips that would apologize, and kiss my
forehead,

because, somehow, someway, I was actually being good
this time.

You've been my audience, my biggest fan, the loudest
mouth in the stands. You started the empty-laundry-soap-
jug-and-rocks-shaker movement at football games. Or maybe,
it was the cowbell movement that you started? Or maybe,
it was both? Hell, I can't remember now, probably because
I got hit in the head to many times… but the whole point
of this matter (and this stanza) is that you made a lot of noise
for us, even if it wasn't actually us who made the tackle,
the catch, the throw, or touchdown. And for that, Maw, we
(and I'm collectively speaking for my other two brothers, here)
Thank you! And we Love you, and Appreciate you, and we
are so lucky to have you as our mother (I'd even admit that
in public)!

Oh! Mother dearest, how art thou so sweet(?) (Is that a question?)

Anyway, Admittedly, this poem has gotten a little out of hand.

But Mother, if so ornery I had not of been,
Then, perhaps it would be so, that we would never
have become… each other's best friend.

Love,
Jacob Paul

Brotherly Love

One of the things in life that we don't have much control over, is who gets to be family and who doesn't. I grew up the middle child of 3 boys, well, unless you take into consideration that my younger brother has always been a bit of a sissy girl, then more like, two-and-a-half boys. But I didn't have any choice in this matter, I didn't get to choose who I wanted to be my brothers (and, well, I'm still angry about that). Being roughly 2.5 years apart from each other, we were more rivals than anything. We fought more than we played, and when we played, we cheated (which is probably one of the reasons why we fought in the first place).

Most of my scars came from my brothers. This isn't even a joke, we "played" hard. I remember (well, kinda) one of the biggest fights that me and my older brother ever had. Hell, I don't remember what it was about… maybe G.I. Joes or something, but I remember that he armed himself with a folded up lawn chair and I picked up a board with a nail poking through it. He swung the chair at my face, the metal corner hitting me just beside the eye, leaving a decent sized gash and knocking me to the floor, and almost over the 10 foot drop-off of the fort that our dad had hand crafted himself. By the time I had realized what had happened, there was already a pool of blood forming on the steps.

I probably didn't cry, because I was more of a hard-ass back then. But either way, the babysitter was in shock and crying when she had to call mom home from work. Mom, understandably, was pissed, but, personally, I thought the stitches were kind of cool.

My younger brother left his mark on my face, too. After a day of playing tennis in the basement with an oil covered tennis ball, we were left to ourselves with soap and water to clean the concrete floors. And by "clean," I mean that we were mostly sliding around and moon-walking in the soapy mess. That is, until my younger brother decided to throw a ball at me and I lost my footing and smacked my chin off of the wet concrete floor. So, another call to mom, another trip to the ER, a special trip to the dentist to fix my chipped tooth and another couple weeks of being grounded (not sure why I was grounded, too… I was mostly innocent), and another scar to remind me that I, in fact, did NOT get to choose who my brothers would be.

This became a very typical kind of childhood for us. From holes being punched into locked doors, and toys being lit into flames, to choke holds and ninja moves; we were more than a handful.

But you see, the truth is, my brothers were my first friends (and first enemies). They were my teammates in baseball, football and basketball. They were who I learned from, who I experienced new things with (even if that included stitches or getting spanked and grounded), and they were, in one way or another, always there when I needed them (because mom and dad made them, but still…).

Here's the thing that brothers often don't think about… no matter how different we are (Jeremy the mechanic, Jason the engineer, and ME the good looking, well mannered, charming, caring, athletic, romantic, intelligent, funny, imaginative, creative, ((did I say good looking??)), writer, hunter, firearms instructor (self-appointed), and friend), no matter what sets us apart… we are STILL very much the same.

We have instilled in us the same drive to help others, to protect others, to love and to do what's right. We were raised up together in a family based on morals and values and character. We share the same type of humor. We have the same blood running through our veins (or spilling out of those brotherly scrapes and cuts). We are the same, no matter if we chose it or not.

Even though I sometimes wish that I was an only child, spoiled by the fruits of my "good behavior" and only-child-cuteness; I can't help but to sit back, think about a boring brotherless life, and appreciate the fact that I had everything a child could ever need growing up, and everything a man could ever ask for, in the loyalty, direction, and love of my brothers.

And eventually, I'm sure that our parents will love them just as much as they love me (because I'm clearly the favorite).

Meh... Christmas

Was it just me, or were there others who found it a little more difficult to get into the Christmas spirit this year?

I don't know if it was the 108 degree weather, here, in Ohio, or maybe the sunburn I got from taking out the trash shirtless the other day, or perhaps, the lack of a special little snow bunny to spoil me this year... but either way, my jingle bells weren't jingling, and it certainly didn't look a lot like Christmas, from here.

To be honest, I've never felt as pathetic as I have this year, when it came to giving out gifts. The lack of money, and time to shop, sent me scouring the house, late Christmas Eve, for something to wrap and hand out on Christmas day.

So, everyone got .22 bullets. I know, how exciting. How pitiful. How tragic. How embarrassing.

I did it to myself, you know… stubbornly chasing dreams and wild ideas of the perfect job. Meanwhile, my wallet, my bank account, and my gift-getters suffered.

But in my Christmas Eve search for something amazing to give, I found something worth more than what money can buy. In the sad, heartbreaking swirl of the last little bit of cheap-tequila-margarita and past Christmas gift ideas, I found a childhood memory.

While thinking about what to give to my deserving mother, I stumbled upon the memory of how excited I used to get, at 12 years old, to read my new poems to my mom. I would burst out of my room, so excited at the crap that I just scribbled into stanzas, and I would interrupt her motherly duties (chores?) just so that she could listen to this *crap*. And God bless her, she acted like she really enjoyed it!

I wanted to capture that memory, in a story, for my mother.

So, at 8:43 pm on Christmas Eve, I swallowed my last little bit of margarita, grabbed a half-empty Gatorade from the fridge, and wrote my mother some stupid, goofy, retro, throwback of a story to when my number one bleacher fan became my number one poetry fan.

And, as I sadly handed out identically shaped, newspaper wrapped, baggies of ammunition, I may have felt a tinge of a tight lipped grin stretch the outer flanks of my cheeks, and possibly, just maybe, felt a small stir of excitement as I watched my mother open her oddly shaped package. And then pull out the small, crayon illustrated book called, Jacob and Maw Become BFF's, and read it out loud.

Jacob and Maw Become BFF's

Once upon a time, there was a very ornery little boy named Jacob. Jacob drove his mother crazy doing some of the most foolish things. Jacob would climb the highest trees and hang from the branches, he would climb up on top of the roof and hide from babysitters, and Jacob would speak out in class and make all of the other kids laugh out loud. Jacob was the class clown.

But one day, probably after receiving 20 lashes from his mother's whip and being confined to his sleeping quarters on half rations and hard labor, Jacob decided to pick up his #2 mechanical pencil, grab a piece of college rule notebook paper, and write down his thoughts and feelings. Jacob was onto something....

He wrote, and wrote, and wrote, and scratched and scribbled out words, and then wrote some more, until he was almost completely satisfied with his work. Then, he picked up his paper, ran to the bottom of his mother's bedroom steps, and yelled, "MAW!! THE MEATLOAF!!" (nonono, that's not what Jacob yelled.) He yelled, "Please, lovely mother, come listen."

And listen, she did. She listened closely. She listened well. And she listened with a smile. She was proud. She knew that Jacob was special… not the "special" kind of special, but actually, truly, special. From then on, whenever Jacob would write something new, he would rush out of his room, with his paper flapping in his hand, and with excitement on his breath, he would read it out loud to his mother.

No matter what she was doing, she would stop, listen, smile, and either, give her approval, or tell Jacob not to use all of those curse words.

But Jacob was stubborn, Jacob was ornery… and Jacob used all of those curse words, anyway. He wrote poem after poem after poem, reading them all to his mother first.

And, like a proud mother, she decided to look passed all of those curse words and ornery references to things that she didn't quite care for, and she instantly became Jacob's BIGGEST FAN.

All of a sudden, Jacob went from being his mother's ornery little shit, to his Maw's favorite son, I mean, poet. The End.

It's not my best work, by any means. It's not attractive, or extravagant, or powerful, or even amazing, but knowing my mother, she would rather have something as silly, and goofy, and from-the-heart like that, than a gift card, or necklace, or brand new car... well, ok, she might rather have a brand new car. But you know what I mean.

And, knowing my mother, she will probably store this away with the other goofy shit that I wrote her or made her, and some day... open it up, pull it out, smile, read it again, maybe laugh... maybe cry... maybe wonder who in the hell I am (who knows). But she will remember a stupid gift like that, some pretty cool memory from my childhood, way more than she would remember something that I bought her.

What I'm trying to say is, even when we feel that we have nothing of value to give, we still do. We will always have a smile, laughter, kindness, some fun memory, or just a small, simple, little gesture that says, "I appreciate you," to offer.

No matter how broke you are, how worthless you feel, or how poor your mood is, you always have the ability to show someone that you care.

Children Laughing

What a strange chaotic noise stirring from the playroom of my mother's house. Just a few years ago

I would have been appalled at the sound of such disaster.

Back then, when my best friends started dating women with kids, it was new and annoying. Hell, I was still a kid; staying out all night chasing a different kind of laughter, a different kind of love. I was living a fast life, where noise only irritated my head.

Laughter. How on earth could something so pure be an inconvenience? How could I let myself fall so far down into that darkness?

Perhaps, it wasn't *their* laughter that was so painful, but the lack of my own...

After all, aren't we supposed to have this life figured out by the time we reach our late 20's? It seemed as though everyone around me had. My friends, all happy and marrying, starting to raise kids of their own. And here I was, still chasing the moon.

The thought of such responsibility scared the shit out of me. I won't deny it. Kids are scary, with their cute little dimples, bright smiles and shitty diapers; how can I raise a child if I'm still trying to raise my head?

Love had been my raft when I was younger. But, so quickly, it had turned and destroyed me. And those demons from my past just wouldn't let me go. I was a step behind, dragging that baggage around like a dead dog behind me. Everything that I thought I knew about happiness kept on leaving me, betraying me, laughing in my face as it walked out the door.

So, of course, I was tainted, jaded, and scared to give happiness a chance.

And then, you three came along, laughing (and at times, screaming, crying, kicking, hitting, throwing, whining) and saved me.

You flashed into my life like a meteor from the far reaches of the galaxy. You hit me, inspired me, moved me, awoke me, and gave me breath.

It is your kids playing in my mother's play room this Christmas, and their joy leads me back to watch them.

Cayton swipes through the toy chest, flipping over nerf guns and tonka trucks. He looks up at me grinning, holding the marshmallow shooter.

"What's this, Jake?" He asks, holding it up to show me.

Aubrey tries to pull it from his hands, and for a moment, I panic at the thought of correcting her.

"Whoa. Whoa. Whoa, little lady. We gotta share."

And she looks up at me scolding in displeasure. I can't help but laugh at the ornery kid who mom says reminds her of me. Then she smiles, giggles, grabs a Barbie and runs out the door laughing.

Cayton is right behind her "bang banging" her with the marshmallow gun, laughing loudly.

I'm not sure how I got so lucky, but I grab a nerf gun from the floor, and with the broadest of smiles, I chase after them giggling.

Ninth Chapter
Wisdom

Where, And Where <u>NOT</u>, To Put Your Penis

I'm a firm believer that owning a penis comes with great responsibility.

Matter of fact, I would even petition that each penis should come with its very own user manual. I mean, let's face it, for those of us who have penises, one of the hardest things to figure out, is what exactly to do with it. I'm completely serious right now (well, kind of). How are we supposed to know where, and where we shouldn't put our penis? It seems that we are left merely to the trial and error of drunken Saturday nights, or the embellished stories of our overly-eager-to-impress friends who want to share with us an easy place where WE could possibly put our penis, too; or we hear from those same friends (who aren't so eager, anymore) to sadly share with us a place where we should not put our penis.

We are simply left to these devices: trial and error, and word of mouth.

Now, as with any loaded gun, proper training and safe handling is required. So, why is it that we are handed this little pea shooter at birth and tossed into the shooting gallery of our teenaged years, without any knowledge of where we should pull the trigger and where we should probably just leave it on safe and put it back into its holster? It's no wonder that we end up with so many misfires and negligent discharges. Hell, we were handed this thing and told to go bag a damn lion. But, how can we slay the king of the jungle when we don't even know how to un-cock our cock? How can we be responsible penis owners when we haven't the slightest idea of where, and where NOT, to put our penis?

Well, luckily, I'm here to help.

Let's imagine for a second that we all had this wise, caring, brilliant, expert-penis-owning father, who sat us down when we were 12 years old and explained to us exactly where we should, and should NOT, put our penis. I would have to imagine that it would go something like this...

Father: "Son, come have a seat here next to me on the bed."

Son: Just starting to learn that he carries with him a God-given loaded weapon, with a seemingly unlimited amount of ammo; sits down nervously beside his father, worried that he might be in trouble for blowing up his brother's GI-Joe's with M-100's. "Yeah, dad?"

Father: A bit nervous himself, just blurts it out. "Let's talk about your penis."
(ok, ok, that's just kinda creepy) Maybe, he says instead… "Son, let's talk about penis responsibility… specifically, where, and where not, to put your penis." (yeah, that's better).

Son: Not weirded out at all (because this is completely fictional and MY damn story) simply says "Okay."

Father (continues): "Well, you know your friend, Jimmy, right? The one who eats earth worms for attention and farts at the dinner table for laughs… well, anything that Jimmy puts his penis into, well son, that is NOT where you should put your penis."

At this point, his son just nods his head in agreement.

Father: "Ok, now… you know Ms. Davis, right?"

Son: "You mean, Loose Ms. Lucy?"

Father: "Uhh, yeeaaahh… her. Son (shaking his head), this is NOT where you put your penis." (thinking) "Matter of fact, as a general rule… anyone with a similar nickname, is NOT where you put your penis."

Son: "But, what about…"

Father: "No, son. Buts will only get you into trouble. And, speaking of BUTTS, son, this is, also, NOT where you put your penis."

His son crinkles his nose in thought… and then nods his head with understanding.

Father: Shifting with awkwardness. "Alright, now… just bear with me on this next place. You know how Uncle Ted sometimes uses the sweeper late at night? Or, you remember that time when we had to rush Uncle Ted to the hospital because he slipped and fell out of the shower and his penis somehow got stuck in a 16oz aluminum beer bottle??! Well… son… (his father looks down, pauses, and then meets his son's anxious gaze), only put your penis in places that were meant for penises, alright?"

They both chuckle at Uncle Ted's expense.

Father: "Now, for some of your friends, they'll learn this the hard way… but, son… never pay someone money to put your penis there. This is NOT where you put your penis, son. And, if you don't believe me, just ask my buddy, Nick, the next time he comes over for drinks… alone."

Son: "The one who's always scratching himself?"

Father: "Yes. Yes, that guy."

Father: "Now, there's one more place that you should NOT put your penis. It's a little difficult to explain, so if there's any questions, just feel free to ask me when I'm done. Well, imagine that it's summer, son. And, you have worked up a pretty powerful thirst ALL day long sitting at the beach. Now, son, you have an unlimited supply of water, the same water that has quenched your thirst for many years. The water that you take with you wherever you go, because, you just enjoy this water so much, son, you love this water… and, well, this water is cold, and crisp, and very satisfying. Son, this water is good. But, on this particular day, you don't want water… on this particular day, you want something with a little more flavor, let's sayyy… juice, son, today you want juice. You with me so far?"

Son: "Uhhh, ok. So, I'm thirsty, and I have water to drink, the same water that I've had for years and I love it, but today I want juice, instead?"

Father: "Yeah. Yeah, exactly. Okay, so you want juice… instead of this perfect water that you've been drinking for so long now. So, you decide that you're not going to drink this perfectly fine water… that you're going to try a sip of this small, tan, skinny, sexy, younger, new juice, instead. Well, son… do NOT take a sip of this juice; this is NOT where you put your penis. Understand?"

His son takes a second to let that sink in, and then nods his head "yes."

His Father goes on: "Now, this might be hard for you to understand, right now (as he pulls out his wallet and removes the high school prom photo of him and his son's mother, and hands it to his son) "Look at this picture real close. Look at me and your mother. Do you see that smile on my face… that spark of life in her eyes? Do you see that ring on her finger? Do you see how close we are? How much we refuse to let any kind of distance between us? Son, can you see all of the happiness and love that's right here in this picture?"

His son looks closely and nods.

Father: Well, son… (he wraps his arm around his son and squeezes him tightly), when you find something like this… something this amazing and magical and incredible, well… son, this is where you can put your penis."

Tips On How To Survive Being Single

The Ebola Virus. Climate Change. World War 3. Massive Earthquakes. Super Volcanoes. The Zombie Apocalypse. And… The SINGLE LIFE.

I've watched, listened, and read on how to survive all of these catastrophes except for the last one. It seems that the mainstream media doesn't care that millions upon billions upon gazzillions of people die daily attempting to survive The SINGLE LIFE. I mean, where is the survival help for the bagillions of people suffering through the cataclysmic meltdown of being single? It's contagious, you know? And, hell, if you ain't careful, you can catch it, too.

So, where does this leave us single folks, besides fighting for our lives???

It leaves us searching… searching for any kind of help whatsoever. I mean, after all, it's not our fault that we're single… it's a worldwide pandemic. And even if you haven't caught this horrible disease yet, even if you're thinking, "oh, no… that'll never happen to me, I'll never catch *The Single Life.*" Well, let me tell ya, the more single people that you expose yourself to, whether it's at the grocery store, the movies or the mall, sooner or later you will probably catch it, too.

But luckily (and heroically), I'm here to help. If you happen to be single now or wake up in the morning feeling a little single, just refer to these survival tips:

How to Survive Being Single

#1. <u>Single Life Survival Kit</u>: Everyone will need a single life survival kit if they plan on making it through being single alive. This kit should include items such as, but not limited to: clean undies to change into when an attractive person is near; a pack of gum and or breath mints so that you can mask the nasty smell of single breath; some sort of body spray or cologne to cover up the rotting romance smell that being single often leaves behind; a high-limit credit card in order to purchase alcoholic medication for you and other single people; and lastly, but most essential; a survival attitude that confidently and boldly says "yes, I will get through this and I will not be just another victim to this crippling disease."

#2. <u>Single Life Survival Candles</u>: To use when the power goes out in your love life. Light these during evening hours while you converse with other single and (hopefully) attractive persons. *Extra tip: use scented single life survival candles as they also fumigate the single life smell from your location.

#3. <u>Group Hobbies</u>: Educate yourself and become familiar with hobbies that can be done with more than one person. The more activities you can do, the greater are your chances in surviving being single.

#4. <u>Public Exposure</u>: I know this may seem counterproductive during a pandemic, but you may find that getting out and about will greatly influence your ability to interact with other infected individuals, which will likely increase your survival rate. **But don't forget your Single Life Survival Kit!

#5. Always Have an Evacuation Plan: For example, you're drinking at a single life gathering establishment and all of a sudden you come into contact with an attractive, fellow-infected, person and you'd like to take them back to your house to administer Single Life First-Aid... make sure that you have a way to evacuate yourself and this other person safely back to your dwelling. ***Once there, it may be appropriate to use a few Single Life Survival Candles, as well.

With a positive mindset and a lot of preparation... you, me, and a handful of others can survive this whole *being single* pandemic.

I Didn't Get A Pony

Well, I didn't get a pony, this year. Matter of fact, I didn't even get a saddle. No rope. No hat. No gun. Hell, I didn't even get a "Yeehaw!"

"What the hell, Santa? I've been good. I brushed my teeth twice a day (well, most days), I used my manners, I said my prayers, I even donated again this year. So Santa, I'm not sure if you're getting lazy or what... but maybe you didn't check your list twice??? I have two names, you know? Jake and Jacob. "Jacob" is usually the one everyone uses when I'm in trouble... so how about next year, you look for "Jake," instead? Thanks, Love Jake."

Okay, so my horse phase only lasted a year or two. But honestly, you know, like most kids (note the sarcasm), for the longest time growing up, all I wanted for Christmas was a sword and ninja stars. Like, the real kind... not all the plastic one's that I was getting. But here's the thing, I wouldn't really remember how badly I wanted them until, well... about 2 weeks before Christmas. In other words, I wouldn't start being "semi-good" until then. Unfortunately (or fortunately, rather), I never got a real sword or real ninja stars until I was 18 and able to buy them on my own.

Look people, don't judge me, I've been a ninja since I was 5 and a half years old. And I'll straight up ninja kick you in the hip (because that's all the higher that I can reach) if you think otherwise.

Moving on.

It took me more than a few years to learn that Christmas wasn't actually about getting all of those things that I was trying so hard (for, like, 5 minutes) to be good for. Yes, it took me a while to understand that Christmas should be more about giving than getting. But look, I don't want to fully commit to that mostly full bandwagon. Because, honestly, while we say that it's all about giving, I have to deeply disagree... folks, Christmas can be just as much about receiving as it can be about giving.

Now, before you boo me and call me a jackass (but not to my face because you know that I'll ninja kick you right in the hip), let me explain…

For me, Christmas is watching as, one by one, family and friends pop through different doors of my mother's house, bearing smiles, and hugs, and handshakes that truly say, "I have missed you, I am glad to see you, and I love you." Receiving this affection and family love, is exactly what Christmas is all about.

You see, Christmas is that feeling you get while you watch with excitement as your mother opens the present that you spent days making yourself because, this year, you just couldn't afford to buy much more than a few wood screws and some paint. It's that smile that lights up her face as she digs through your old gun box and those crumpled up newspapers that you used to wrap the present that she now proudly holds up and displays for the rest of the room to see. It's the appreciation and love that comes pouring out of her knowing that all you could wrap for Christmas this year was a hand-made wooden name plaque with shotgun shells and bullet casings representing each child and grandchild that she has. It's the understanding that shows through in the underlining of her smile of what it's like to have a Christmas where you struggle. It's that hug and kiss she gives you because she loves what you made for her and would have loved whatever you would have put into that old beat up cardboard gun box, because the best present that you could have given her, was just simply being there.

It's the mouthwatering smell of your dad's house and the taste of the feast that he and your stepmother prepared. It's that belly busting full feeling that stays with you the rest of the day. And it's the laughter that you all share, because dad gets a little embarrassing with the baby talk around your 1 year old nephew.

Christmas is catching my Grandma and Grandpa taking a break together on the couch from the loud crowd of laughing, drinking, and story-telling family and friends that filled my mother's house Christmas night. It's seeing the golden opportunity for a picture with them as they open the same kind of present that I made for everyone else. It's getting that same exact smile and appreciation that each one of your family members gave you when they opened their presents that you had to make, instead of buy, this year. It's receiving that hug, that warmth of love that lets you know just how special you really are to them.

It's watching and listening to your cousin and brother play guitar and sing as your family drinks and laughs the night away.

It's a room full of love and acceptance for the "new friend" that you brought with you this Christmas (even though your 7 yr. old cousin says that you have too many "new friends" and that they all break up with you, anyway). But, it's, also, that kiss that your "new friend" asks if she can give to you in front of them because, for some reason, half a song in harmony and the numerous wrong-word-back-up-singers, along with the hot (too hot) crackling fireplace, just sets the mood.

Christmas is being the last ones up; you, your "friend", your mom and your stepdad... drinking outdated margaritas with the tequila that your brother got you, talking about the good times, the hard times, and laughing at all the rest...

No, I didn't get a pony, or a sword, or ninja stars... But what I did get, is a very loving, caring, understanding, hilarious, entertaining, talented and accepting family that knows how to give, how to let you receive, how to let anyone or everyone receive the gift of love. You see, Christmas is truly about both giving and receiving love. It's about all of those moments and memories that you create with the people that you love, that you will hold onto, and that you will cherish for as long as you possibly can.

Speaking From A Burnt Tongue

Wisdom, in its infant stages, is nothing more than ignorance and courage.

Lately, I've spent a lot of time wondering where I fit in in this world. And, if that wasn't such a damned cliché, then I would actually feel somewhat philosophical about the whole thing. But the truth is, who hasn't wondered where they belong before? I mean, here I am, 29 years old, I'm in the 2nd or 3rd best shape of my life, I almost have a real Bowflex body, I'm single, looking for a "good" job and contemplating the meaning of life. Let's face it, where we want to be and where we end up, are seldom the same place.

So, where do I want to be? Well, honestly... hell if I know. I mean, how should I know? To my knowledge, this is the first time that I've ever been alive, so how am I, or anyone else for that matter, supposed to have any inkling of an idea of where they want to be?

Wait... happy, right?

We want to be HAPPY. I mean, the people who like nice things, want money; the people who fancy romance (me), want love; those who love to control, want power; and so on and so on. But, seriously, does anyone really know what they want out of life? Hell, I figure we could argue about that for a good 32 minutes or so, but I don't have enough energy nor enough beer to listen to you tell me what you think you know....

Whoa, whoa, whoa... I'm getting a little off track here. This is my point... wisdom. The knowledge of what is true or right coupled with just judgment. It's the insight into the "why we did that" or the "why didn't we do that." It's the reason that you don't dial the numbers scribbled onto bathroom stalls, it's exactly why you should always make and hide a spare key, or the reason that I stopped dating redheads.

It's wisdom that will lead us to where we want to be. In other words, it's experience, it's mistakes, it's bumpy roads that let us know how much we need a new suspension. In essence, we learn as we go.

Alright, so they say that we should learn from our mistakes; to get up after we fall down, to bend but not break. They say that there's a lesson inside the pain, that we cannot have the good without the bad, the right without the wrong.

Well, I say…

Go skinny dipping every chance that you get. Kiss her. Kiss her. KISS HER! Learn to start a fire, but still bring a blanket. Learn to whisper… a loud mouth drowns out a soft song. Touch her… not inappropriately, well, I mean, unless she wants you to… but, I'm saying touch her face, her back, her shoulders, her neck, her leg and most importantly, her hand. Take a dare. Give a dare. Run, if not for fun, then out of fear… of getting fat. Chase someone, not like a creeper or with a knife, but through the yard and with love. Take the time to say your manners. Give respect. Earn respect. Smile. Laugh. Laugh again. And again. Keep laughing. Never stop laughing. Play as hard as you can, as often as you can. Stop working so much, one thing that I can positively tell you, is that we were not blown breath into our souls just to work our lives away. Spend your money, save your money, and find the right balance between both. Write, sing, dance, draw, EXPRESS yourself. And finally, Love. Love with all you have. Each time, every time. No matter how many times it hurts you. Love for the sake of humanity, love for your children, for their children and love for those who loved before you.

Because without love, the most powerful force on Earth… is hate.

Interview

Interview With Jacob Paul Patchen

Where do you pull your inspiration from when you write?

To be completely honest (because we're all friends here), my inspiration can come from anywhere. Most of the time, a simple thought trickles down into the deep, thrashing waters of the river that I call my mind, and it gets swept away in the torrents of my imagination, tumbling, turning, and banging into everything until it comes gushing out and down the water fall that I call my mouth, and splatters onto paper in the form of words.

These thoughts come to me from a scenic view in nature, from music, from love, passion or heartbreak, and from the awkward or funny situations that I find myself in daily... like, trying to talk to taller women and suddenly realizing that I'm standing on my tippy-toes. (Hell, I just can't win.)

How often do you write?

Well, that's kind of hard to say (because it's c-17 classified). The truth is, it varies. When I was working full time at jobs that I didn't really want to be doing in the first place, I would write whenever I had the opportunity, which, again, varied. I was happy if I was writing a poem every couple weeks or so.

When I was in college, I was writing a lot (obviously, that was my major... well, besides drinking). I would write something creative almost daily. Now, it wasn't always good, but that's besides the point. To be a good writer, you have to write both good and bad pieces. It's just like anything else, you have to learn from your mistakes.

Now, I do something with writing almost every day. On uncreative days, I submit poetry to contests and publishers. On creative days, I write a poem or a blog post. It's sort of that simple.

What do you do when you realize that you have written a piece that you would consider *bad*?

Well, I have a complete meltdown. I trash my house, my truck, and bad talk the elderly… to their face! Then, I go on huge, bank-account-draining shopping sprees until I feel better about myself.

NO. Actually, I usually laugh if it's a poem. Because, like I said earlier: to be a good writer, you have to write both good AND bad pieces. So, I appreciate my effort in translating some thought into words, but I also acknowledge that what I just wrote was CRAP! And then I move on.

Who were your favorite writers growing up? Who did you Idolize?

This is sort of embarrassing… but, I hated to read growing up. When I was forced to read (like, in class) I would read the Goosebumps books, the Hardy Boys books(??), and I remember enjoying 2 other books during my entire childhood… Call of the Wild and Hatchet (and I'm not 100% sure that I finished either of them). But, other than that… I usually just sat there and day dreamed about what we were having for lunch, how cute Kristine looked in that outfit today, or what practice was going to be like after school. The only real writing that I truly enjoyed reading…

was my own. I suppose, because I was fully invested and really connected with the author. Wink Wink.

As for idols… ummm, no one in the writing field. But, let me tell ya, I could mirror Jim Carrey line for line in most of his movies. ALLLLLRRIIGHTY THEN!?

Out all of your writing (poetry, blogs, stories) what is your favorite piece?

Hmm, it's hard to really pick a favorite. I'm not really good at this. But first and foremost, I am a Poet. My poetry is like my firstborn child. It's special. And I've had nearly 20 published so far, but a couple of poems jump out at me right away just because they are memorable, *Wisdom of the Night* and *Mortar Us*.

Wisdom of the Night is a poem that I wrote completely in my head while standing in formation early one morning during boot camp, as we were preparing for a 5 mile hump. I was inspired by the huge full moon glowing orange and bright just before dawn. Now, I had to repeat this poem in my head for about 2 hours until I had the chance to jot it down on some scrap paper. It's nothing extraordinary in meaning… but the entire process was something that I will always remember.

Mortar Us is a poem that I wrote towards the end of my college years, as I was really starting to put my

Iraq experience to paper. It's a longer poem about what it was like to be mortared, bombed, and rocketed on a daily basis, and how it burned a hatred into my heart for the insurgents that would bomb us and then run and hide. Guerrilla Warfare at its finest.

My book, Life Lessons from Grandpa and His Chicken Coop: A Playful Journey Through Some Serious Sh*t, is extremely important to me because it is the book that started this journey. It is the book that opened the world to my writing style, my childhood, my family, and those damn chickens.

How would you describe your writing style?

Well, very conversational. I add frequent little quips and (in my humble opinion) semi-witty one liners every now and then. I think that it keeps the tone light, real, honest, and lets the reader feel like they are sitting right there with me, engaged in conversation. My goal is to use common, everyday language to my advantage. I kind of don't enjoy reading all that much, and I keep that in mind when I write.

I would also say that my style uses a very philosophical approach. I ask a lot of questions because I'm always trying to find some sort of answers. I want my readers to walk away with a different way of thinking. I want them to be inspired, to be moved, to be emotional; I want them to feel my words as though they were just as real as blades or kisses.

What's next?

Well, actually I spent most of last year finishing my first poetry book, Of Love and War, which is about exactly what it says… love and war. It is currently being sent out to publishers and contests.

I will continue to update my blog and author page Jacobpaulpatchen.com, as well.

About The Author

Jacob Paul Patchen was born and raised outside of Byesville, Ohio where he spent his youth tormenting babysitters and hiding in trees. Patchen earns his inspiration through experience, where he writes abundantly about love, war, sex, family and drinking. Jacob is a poet, blogger, an author, and combat veteran.

Check out his 5 star rated debut book on Amazon.com!

Life Lessons from Grandpa and His Chicken Coop: A Playful Journey Through Some Serious Sh*t

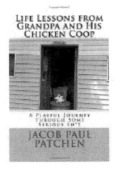

Or pick up some of his poetry in:

GFT Presents: <u>One in Four Vol. 1 Issue 2</u>
- To be the Westward Sky at Sunset
- We Sleep with Mice and Vipers

Veterans Writing Project: <u>0-Dark-Thirty, Fall 2016</u>
　　　- Dying in the Light

Shipwreckt Books: <u>Lost Lake Folk Opera Vol. 4 No.1</u>
　　　- Mortar Us
　　　- Pistol on my Nightstand
　　　- On seeing the Ginger from across the bar
and Hoping that She's Easy

<u>The Deadly Writers Patrol Issue 12</u>
　　　- Lime Trees in Paradise
　　　- Throwing Rocks at the Shitter and Me
　　　- Of Love and War (poem)

Made in the USA
Columbia, SC
10 March 2018